AF199910

Richard Deiss

The Cathedral of the Winged Wheel and the Sugar Beet Station

Trivia and Anecdotes on 222 Railway Stations in Europe

Address of the Author:
Machnower Str 65
D-14165 Berlin
Email: richard.deiss@gmail.com

Pictures on the cover: Amsterdam Station
Inside: old station of S-Hertogenbosch (Wikipedia)
Back: Dijon Station

Publishing: Books on Demand GmbH, Norderstedt
Second English edition, 2020, Originalausgabe

Printed in Germany

ISBN   978-3-751-9970-65

Bibliografische Information der Deutschen Nationalbibliothek
Die Deutsche Nationalbibliothek verzeichnet diese
Publikation in der Deutschen Nationalbibliografie;
detaillierte bibliografische Daten sind im Internet über
http://dnb.d-nb.de abrufbar

Content

5. Southern Europe

6. Central and Eastern Europe

7. South Eastern Europe

8. Russia and Ukraine

9. Caucasus

Preface

This is the translation into English of the European volume of my five-volume series on railway stations worldwide. Each book contains trivia, interesting facts, and anecdotes on about 200 stations. In total, 1001 stations are covered in the five books. Currently, four out of five volumes are available in English, while all five are available in German

In this volume 222 short stories, facts, trivia and anecdotes on railway stations in wider Europe, including Turkey, the Caucasus and Russia are covered. Railway stations in Germany and the Alpine countries are dealt with in separate volumes. The book travels through Europe from North to West and from South to East.

The annex includes some tables with statistical data and other information in table form.

Anecdotes relating to famous people or to dramatic events involving other people are marked with a star (★).

Comments on the content and tips for further stories are appreciated and will be included in the next edition which is foreseen for 2021.

I would like to thank Hubert Riedle (Bern) and Jörg Berkes (Langen) for tips on the content and Nick Snipes (Berlin) for editing the English translation of the book.

Berlin, September 2020
Richard Deiss

1. Northern Europe

1.1 Sweden

★ Vassijaure and the bullet hole

Seven km from the Norwegian border along the Kiruna-Narvik ore railway, lies the Vassijaure station. On 20 May 1940, Sven Sjöberg, a young ranger, waited on the platform for a letter that should come by train. Suddenly, a German aircraft appeared, which flew at low altitude towards the train station. Since the Germans had previously occupied Norway and it was a station near the border, it was equipped to protect the border, and even an armored train was stationed there. Sjöberg opened fire on the plane. The Germans responded, and Sjöberg was hit. Seriously injured, he was taken by train to Kiruna but died during the trip. The next day, mail for Sjöberg arrived at the station. It was a letter permitting him to leave the service to help his parents on their farm. At the news of his death, his mother collapsed and never recovered. The station still has the bullet holes from the exchange of fire between the Germans and Sjöberg, and there is a commemorative plaque on the platform.

Kiruna

The northern Swedish city of Kiruna lives through mining. However, the hollowed out ground leads to cuts and subsidence and more and more damage to buildings. Therefore, a decision was made in 2012 to move the city four km to a safe slope. The moving of the town started in 2014 but is still far from complete. One of the first buildings to move was the railway station of Kiruna, and a new provisional station was built in 2013 at the northeast end of the town. The old station was demolished in 2017.

☞ There are also other unusual things happening in the area. In the vicinity (in Jukkasjärvi), there is an ice hotel, which is rebuilt every winter. Additionally, the British entrepreneur Richard Branson wants to build a "Spaceport" for space tourists near Kiruna. Furthermore, there is a station of the Space Agency ESA located there.

Stockholm CS

In front of the Stockholm Central Station, there is a statue, not for a king, but for the engineer Nils Ericson (1802-1870). He was so instrumental in the construction of the railroad in the country, that he can almost be regarded as "the father of Swedish Railway." Shortly before the completion of the railway station in 1871, Ericson died. The train station's façade has hardly changed since then, but the same cannot be said about the interior. The vaulted hall, where steam engines once were puffing off, now is a waiting room. The train station has also changed from a terminal to a station with through traffic. The station compound also includes a bus station and the Swedish World Trade Center. From the outset, this extension was designed to optimize energy consumption. Overall, only fifteen percent of the compound's energy consumption comes from municipal utilities, and it sometimes even feeds energy into the urban district heating system. The low energy usage is achieved by, among other things, a domed transparent roof, which captures energy and also helps cool the complex in the summer. In wintertime, heat energy is even obtained from the 25,000 people, who pass daily through the World Trade Center. Due to the success of this idea in the trade center, the station operating company Jernhusen wanted to apply the same method in the station proper. Additionally, the organizers of the complex announced in spring 2008 that they also wanted to use the heat energy captured from the approximately about

200,000 passers-by daily in the station to heat a 13-story office building at the station. Up to 15 percent of the energy expended on heating the building is expected to be obtained via that method.

In the ground floor of the Stockholm train station, there is a circular opening, through which one can look at the deeper level. The locals have nicknamed the opening "spittoon (spottkoppen)."

Laholm - the little house on the prairie

When the railway line Malmö-Gothenburg was straightened for high-speed railway traffic, the town of Laholm got a new railway station on the new route. The new station building, a small brick house, is, however, of very modest appearance. Since it is also located three kilometers from the town center, it was popularly nicknamed "The Little House on the Prairie (Lilla huset in het Prairie)," inspired by an American TV series of the same name.

Malmö and the UFO

In 2000, the Öresund fixed link was opened, connecting Copenhagen and Malmö by rail. However, at Malmö Central, trains have to turn around and then travel around the city to reach the bridge. Therefore, a city tunnel was constructed to make Malmö Centralen a train station through traffic and to introduce more stops. The most important new station along the route is the underground station Triangeln (40,000 passengers daily) situated on a triangular square. From street level, passers-by can see the glass dome of light of the station Triangeln. Due to the appearance of the lens-shaped roof, a local newspaper wrote in March 2010, just after the station's opening, that "a UFO landed in the middle of Malmö."

1.2 Norway

Oslo - the station of Tiger Town

In front of Oslo Central Station is the bronze sculpture of a tiger. In recent years, Oslo searched for an icon, and tigers currently have a positive connotation. Economically successful countries are today - or at least before the 2008 financial crisis - called Tigers. Some examples include Iceland (the Arctic Tiger) and Finland (the Nordic Tiger). However, in the 19th century, the term tiger had a different meaning when describing Oslo. Back then, the living conditions were still difficult (think of Knut Hamsun´s 1890 novel *Hunger*). The city was considered so merciless that the writer Bjørnsterne Bjørnson "Tiger Town" in an 1870 poem. Later, this former critical term established itself as the nickname of the city. Oslo then still belonged to Denmark and was called Christiania (also Kristiania starting in 1878). Back then, the main station was still the Eastern Station (adjacent to it, a modern central station was built and opened in 1980). In 1925, the old name of the city, Oslo, was restored. Despite the nation's oil boom since the 1990s, more beggars (Tigger in Norwegian) stayed on the station square. Oslo has, therefore, been derisively called "Tigger City."

Hell frozen over

On the line from Trondheim to Bodo, there is a railway station called Hell. In English, conductors announce upon approaching the station, "Next stop: Hell." On the station premises is a goods shed with the words "Gods Expedition (goods expedition)," which adds some more biblical humor to the mix. In winter, the station is often covered by snow and ice, which might lead some to remark "Hell frozen over."

Finse 1222

A special station, Finse 1222 is also located on the Bergen railway line. It is 1222.2 meters above sea level and the highest railway station in Northern Europe. Not far from the train station one can find a hotel named *Finse 1222*.

Trondheim and the synagogue

Trondheim is situated north of the 63rd latitude. The geographical location leads to several alleged records. With the Grakallen line, Trondheim has the northernmost tramway in the world. The first train station in Trondheim, located on the waterfront in the Kalvskinnet district, is now home to what is believed to be the world's northernmost synagogue. However, the actual record holder is found in Murmansk, Russia. In reality, the Synagogue of Trondheim, which was established there after the small Jewish community of the city purchased the disused railway station in 1925, is only the fifth-northernmost in the world.

☞ Trondheim was an important center of Christian pilgrimage in Northern Europe during the Middle Ages because canonized King Olav II is buried in the Trondheim Cathedral. The town was once called "Jerusalem of the North."

Trondheim and the landslide

In 1877, a new train station was built in Trondheim on an artificial island in the harbor to ensure good connections to navigation. However, the newly created terrain was not stable. In April 1888, the ground gave way, there was a landslide, and 180 meters of track were swallowed by the sea. The station was renamed three times due to the city's frequent name changes. When the station opened, the city was called Throndhjem, later it changed to Trondheim, andthen Nidarors. In 1931, the city was renamed Trondheim.

1.3 Denmark

Copenhagen - the InterRailers Paradise

In the 1980s, when many young people travelled with the Interrail pass, the main railway station of Copenhagen (built in 1911) had a good reputation amongst them. It was the first railway station, which had a special InterRailers travel centre, with cooking possibilities, showers, and an info-centre. Yet, the station is not only a meeting point for InterRailers; even Copenhageners tell each other, "we meet at the station clock (møo mig under uret)."

Hoje Taastrup

The station of the Copenhagen suburb Hoje Taastrup was opened in 1986. The station building above the tracks, which became the symbol of the community, gave rise to a pun due to its three arches. Because of its station, Hoje Taastrup is called "Buernes By (City of Arcs)," which almost sounds like "Byernes By (City of Cities)." At the south end of the station complex is Thor's Tower. At 26 meters tall, it the tallest sculpture in Scandinavia.

Aarhus

A common stereotype is that Copenhageners think they live in the only big city in Denmark. They joke about the long-distance trains' name, "Intercity," since there is only one city in the country. The Copenhageners also like to make jokes about the Jutlanders or the inhabitants of Aarhus. One goes like this: "Why do the Aarhusers remove the doors from bathrooms? So no one can look through the key-hole." Does this also apply to the Aarhus Central Station? With 17,000 passengers and about 30,000 users per day, it is the busiest Danish railway station outside Copenhagen.

Køge Nord and the new station hose

Køge Nord station, which was opened in May 2019, links the new high-speed Copenhagen-Ringsted line with the suburban train lines, various cycle paths, and a motorway. In cities with stronger nickname traditions, such as London, Rotterdam, or Berlin, the long pedestrian walkway would have long since been known as the tube, millipede, or rectum. In Denmark, however, there is still no mention of a nickname. It is to be hoped that in the long-term that vandalism and wear and tear will not turn the pathway into a "long misery."

★ Elsinore and Hamlet

In the city of Helsingør, lies the fortress Kronberg. Kronberg is also called Hamlet Castle because the hero and namesake of William Shakespeare's *Hamlet* lives in this fortress. As soon as you leave the city's station, you come across a bronze statue of Hamlet on the left of the portal and a statue of his lover Ophelia on the right. The Danish sculptor Rudolph Tegner created the pair in 1937. In 1938, they were placed in a park near Marienlyst Castle, where Mayor Christensen wanted to establish a Hamlet Museum. For this purpose, a plan was made for three additional statues of the three most important characters of the play plus a statue of Shakespeare himself. However, only the two statues were ever realized. In 1980, they were removed from the park and stored in a depot. In 1983, they were placed in the city centre, and in 1996, they moved near the castle. Due to construction work, they had to move again in 2008, and this time, they were placed by the railway station, where they are still standing today.

1.4 Finland

Helsinki Central Station - the station with giants

In 1904, a competition to design a new station was announced in Helsinki. The winner was the young architect Eliel Saarinen (1873-1950) with his National-romantic design in neo-Romanesque style. However, this sparked a debate in which critics argued for more modern designs. Finally, Saarinen radically re-worked his design towards a more modern and clearer Art Nouveau architecture.

The station has a 50 square meter waiting lounge, which was originally built specifically for the Russian Tsar. When the station was opened in 1919, Finland was no longer part of Russia. Therefore, the waiting lounge was reserved for the President of Finland. The station name was written in two languages: Finnish and Swedish. The clear design of the station, with a mighty clock tower, its pink granite, and the giant holding lamps still impress today. In 1923, its architect Eliel Saarinen emigrated to the US. His son, Eero Saarinen was famous for the construction of the TWA terminal at John F. Kennedy Airport in New York.

☞ In addition to the main station of the Helsinki, the Art Nouveau train station built in 1905 in the town of Kajaani has also been called the most beautiful train station in Finland.

Nokia - the unassuming station

The Nokia Company was founded in 1865 in the small town of Nokia, Finland. Once, the company manufactured paper products and rubber boots. Around 2010 more than 1 billion people worldwide used Nokia phones. Often, foreign tourists visiting Finland make a trek especially to Nokia. There, however, they are disappointed to find no high-tech station, but only a few platforms and no station building.

☞ There is also a Nokia station in Bochum, Germany, however, the Nokia factory there (after which the station was named) has been closed.

★ Once in a lifetime to Inari

In the summer of 1998, the movie *Trains'n'Roses* (*Zugvögel ...Einmal nach Inari* in German) was released in German cinemas. The director was Peter Lichtefeld. The protagonist Hannes (played by Joachim Krol) is a beer delivery van driver in Dortmund, Germany. He spends lots of time thinking about railway timetables. He wants to participate in the railway timetable competition in the Northern Finnish town of Inari. Hannes packs his bags and applies for paid leave. Yet, a new boss arrives and does not want to let Hannes go. Hannes freaks out, knocks the boss out, and sets out on a train journey to the Arctic circle. The irony of the story: Inari, located on Lake Inari in Lapland, is in reality far from any railway line and therefore has no station. From the train station of Kemijärvi, where a train only arrives once a day, the protagonist must, therefore, continue traveling by bus to Inari. Lichtefeld supposedly got the idea for the film in 1994 on a return trip by train from Sodankylä to Helsinki. However, even in Sodankylä itself, there is no train station.

The train robbers of Humppila

In 1973, the station of Humppila burned down. Burglars had tried to break open the safe of the nearby post office. When they heard noises, they left in a hurry, but let the welding torches with open flames on the ground. Thus, not only did the post office burn down but also the neighboring railway station. Ten years later, a new function railway station building was finished.

The station of Kolari

The station of Kolari is the northernmost of the Finnish Railways. From here, there is more than 1,060 km of track to the main train station of Helsinki. Kolari lies in Lapland on the border with Sweden and is connected by a branch line to the border station of Tornio. Kolari's station building, which was finished in 2000, has a conic roof element that mimics the style of a Lappish hut. Lappish huts have such roofs, to allow smoke to escape. The station of Kolari is often busy in the winter season when many skiers from the south of the country arrive here.

★ Mannerheim's saloon car in Mikkeli

During the Second World War, Mikkeli in eastern Finland was the headquarters of the Finnish army. The lounge car, with which Field Marshal Carl Gustaf Emil Mannerheim travelled almost 80,000 km through Finland between 1939 and 1946, is on display at the station of Mikkeli. It can be visited each year on the 4th of June (Mannerheim's birthday).

Mannerheim's salon car in the station of Mikkeli

★ Littonen and Lenin

In 1907, the Russian revolutionary Vladimir Lenin tried to flee from Finland to Sweden. At that time, Finland still belonged to Russia. He took a train in a suburb of Helsinki to Turku. From there, he was supposed to travel by boat. However, while on the train, Lenin believed he was being pursued by two members of the Tsar's secret police. To shake off his pursuers, Lenin jumped off at Littonen station just before the train arrived at Turku. Lenin got slightly injured but was able to continue to the Port of Turku. By the time he arrived, the steamboat to Sweden had already departed. With the help of sympathizers, Lenin successfully found refuge on the island archipelago located between Finland and Sweden. Later, he took a boat from there to Sweden. From Sweden, Lenin finally travelled through Germany before arriving in Switzerland, his place of refuge. Today, a plaque in Littonen station reminds passers-by of Lenin's jump from the train.

★Lahti and Lenin again

In the spring of 1917, Lenin returned to St. Petersburg by train after travelling through Switzerland, Germany, Sweden, and Finland. The Russian revolution was then underway, and Germany provided Lenin with tickets and visas. German leadership believed that a revolution lead by Lenin would weaken Russia. However, the traditional Russian forces once more got the upper hand, and Lenin had to flee from Russia for the last time in July 1917. Dressed as a fireman, he left on a locomotive heading toward Helsinki. However, in the station of Lahti, Lenin had to get off. The heat of the steam engine had melted the wax that held the mask, revealing his easily recognizable face.

The splendid railway station of Haapsalu (Estonia)

Haapsalu is a resort town on the western coast of Estonia. The royal family chose the town as their summer resort, In 1905, the railway line St. Petersburg-Tallinn (Reval) was extended to Haapsaluin. Therefore, the town needed a representative train station. Finally, a very elongated railway station was built. The longest covered platform in Europe (216 m) protected passengers, such as the Tsar family, against wind and weather. The station complex also contained a pavilion for the royal family. On the 100th birthday of the railway line in 1995, the train service to Haapsalu was decommissioned. Since 1997, after being renovated in the original style, the station houses the Estonian Railway Museum.

Bahnhof Haapsalu (der linke Flügel beherbergt das Museum)

17

★ The station of Riga, the Russian pop duo

Today, the train stations of the Baltic States have limited passenger numbers due to competition from buses, cars, and airplanes and changes to the flow of traffic after the break up of the Soviet Union. One exception to this trend is the main station of Riga, where over 25 million passengers passed through in 2006. In May 2003, the station had some prominent travelers. The Russian pop duo Tatu was participating in the Euro Vision Song Contest in Riga and came from Moscow.

On the backside of the station are the station market halls, which were installed in the former Zeppelin hangars erected by the German military during World War I.

☞ In Soviet times, the station tower had a digital clock, which was replaced by an analog one during a renovation.

Valga / Valka

On the Latvia-Estonia border lies two similarly named cities. On the Estonian side is Valga and on the Latvian side lies Valka. Valga/Valka was once a city. However, after the First World War and the collapse of the Russian Empire, the city was claimed by both Estonia and Latvia. Finally, the British Commissioner for the Baltic States Sir Stephen Tallents decided to make a neutral judgment. Tallents proposed to divide the city along the local river. Thus, the larger northern part of the city—with the train station—became a part of Estonia under the name of Valga, and the part south of the river was given to Latvia as Valka. As the Baltic states were annexed by the Soviet Union, the border between the two towns disappeared again. In 1949, the station was generously (in a style that is reminiscent of Weinbrenner buildings in Karlsruhe, Germany) rebuilt. In 1991, the Baltic States became independent again, and the city was strictly separated following the guidelines of Tallent's earlier decision. Fences were erected in the city, and people faced detention for illegal crossing. However, since the two countries became part of the Schengen area in December 2007, border controls disappeared again. The station is now the only international rail traffic connection between the two countries.

Vilnius Airport Railway

In a blog about airports, a blogger stated that Vilnius's airport has the atmosphere of a railway station. Since October 2008, this is not quite wrong because the airport of the Lithuanian capital received its own airport railway station with connections. This made the Vilnius airport railway station the first airport station of the Baltics.

Vilnius Airport train station

Vilnius Central Station

The Soviet Union once had the highest number of metro and tram systems in the world. And while Lithuania was part of the Soviet Union for 45 years, the capital Vilnius has no subway or tramways. Due to increasing motor vehicle traffic in the densely built downtown and the city's desire to become a true metropolis, there are plans to build a subway in the future. The time of the rail-free urban transport in the city was also been shortened by the opening of a funicular-like inclined lift from downtown to Gediminas Castle in 2003.

In the hall of Vilnius's central station, a model of the train station in HO scale is shown that includes an already completed subway. Another strange anomaly about the model is that the locomotives parked in the station carry the Deutsche Bahn (Germany Railways) logo (DB). Even if the DB would like to have trains in Lithuania, their locomotives could not drive on the broad-gauge network of Lithuanian railways.

A second model rail landscape on the concourse shows another strange scene. An ICE (Inner City Express, another train type from DB) high-speed train sits in a landscape that is intended to represent Lithuania, which is also ironic since the houses in the model are in the style of cabins from the Alps. The only change made to the ICE train is the Lithuanian railway LG being placed over the DB logo. The Lithuanian railway network for a long time was part of the Russian and Soviet network, which is also evident in the built model railway's landscape. The terminal loops of the miniature train network are located in Belarus and Kaliningrad.

Model of Vilnius station in the main station hall

Kupiskis

Originally, the Lithuanian city of Kupiskis was supposed to get a station near the city centre. However, the city did not want to make a payment (a kind of bribe) to the railway company to facilitate their work. Thus, the railway company built the railway station far from the center. As a result, the city's residents must walk far or catch a cab to reach the station.

Marijampoles beautiful railway station

The railway station of the Lithuanian city of Marijampole was built in 1923. The newly independent state wanted to add architectural character to the station. Therefore, the station got a high clock tower and Art Nouveau overtones. In the Second World War, Marijampole was heavily damaged. However, the station remained intact and is now one of the few architectural attractions of the city.

★ Sugihara and visa at the station of Kaunas

In 1939, Chiune Sugihara became the Japanese vice-consul of the Japanese Consulate in Kaunas, Lithuania. In 1940, many Jews from Poland, where they were threatened by the German occupiers, tried to get an exit visa. At the time, the Soviet Union occupied Lithuania. Hundreds of refugees came to the Japanese consulate to apply for a visa to Japan, where there was a Jewish community in Kobe, and to where there was access to the country via the Transsiberian Railway. However, the Japanese Government provided visas only to people with sufficient means or with a transit visa of a third country. Yet, the queues at the consulate were getting longer. Thus, Sugihara, after consulting his wife, decided in July 1940 to break the rules and to issue visas on his own. These visas included a 10-day transit visa for Japan. Every day he worked 18-20 hours and issued visas, which saved the lives of thousands of Jews. Yet, the Japanese government did not approve of Sugihara's behaviour and closed the consulate in September of 1940 and forced Sugihara to leave for Germany. However, Sugihara continued to issue visas in his train compartment while waiting at the station of Kaunas. As the train to Berlin set in motion, Sugihara had to throw the visa paperwork and visa stamps from the train window to the platform so that they could still be useful for the refugees. After Kaunas, Sugihara served as Consul General in Prague, Königsberg, and Bucharest. In Bucharest, he fell into Russian custody. However, he left in 1946 on the Trans-Siberian Railway to Japan.

2. Benelux

2.1 The Netherlands- the Randstad

Amsterdam´s station foundation

The Amsterdam Central Station is the busiest railway station in the Netherlands (150,000 travelers and 100,000 visitors per day). It was built in 1881-1889 by the architect Pierre Cuypers in a similar style as the Rijksmuseum of the city. The station was built on three small islands in the IJsselmeer, which were made from sand, which had been moved for the construction of the North Sea Canal. Additionally, 8687 stakes were driven into the ground to obtain a stable foundation. The building still sagged a little at first, which led to delays. The station actually blocks the view of the Ijsselmeer. Its main portal looks like a gate, to show that this is the new way in and out of the city. On the east wing of the station, one can find the Royal Pavilion, complete with parking for carriages.

Amsterdam CS and its copies

While Rotterdam and The Hague have brutalist concrete building Central Stations, Amsterdam has one of the most beautiful station buildings in Western Europe. It is, therefore, no surprise that its architecture has been copied several times. For example, the architecture of Tokyo's main train station is said to have been inspired by the Amsterdam train station. After the damages of the Second World War, the similarity is, however, not obvious today. Greater similarity can be seen between the station and the Ana Hotel at the Huis ten Bosch Holland theme park near Nagasaki. The Amsterdam station was the model for this hotel, but the Japanese added a few more floors to the design to accommodate more guests. A nearly perfect copy of the station could be found in Holland Village in Shenyang in northeastern China. In 2000, the Amsterdam main train station was copied perfectly in a 1:1 scale there as a restaurant, but the building was knocked down by 2009.

The beautiful railway station of Haarlem

On the 20th of September, 1839, a train heading towards Haarlem left Amsterdam. The train was expected to make the 16 km journey in approximately 30 minutes time. As was the case for the first German train between Nuremberg and Fürth, the locomotive was named Eagle (Dutch de Arend). Thus, the railway age in the Netherlands had begun. Haarlem railway station was originally made of wood, but, a few years later, a handsome railway station was built in the neoclassical style. Yet, at the beginning of the 20th century, the railway line in the city was raised to not obstruct traffic, and a new train station had to be built.

Between 1905 and 1908, the new station was built according to the plans of the architect D.A.N. Margadant. The only Art Nouveau station of the Netherlands, Haarlem's station is revered by connoisseurs as the most beautiful in the country. Already at the opening one did not want to disturb the "paradise." For passengers who came from the nearby psychiatric hospital, there was a separate waiting room.

Leiden Station

As in many other Dutch cities, the university city of Leiden's railway tracks were raised above ground level during the 1950s to reduce traffic congestion. Hence, a new station building needed to be built. However, due to the station's gray concrete post-war architecture, it was not popular with the population. Soon after, the phrase "as ugly as the train station Leiden (zo lelijk as het station van Leiden)" came into circulation. In the following decades, traffic grew due to the increasing number of students in the city, and the reception building became too small. Finally, the gray concrete station was torn down and replaced with a light, airy, glass and steel construction, which was opened in 1996. Yet, the city still was not satisfied. Since Leiden ranked fifth on the list of busiest stations, the city wanted to have the station classified as "CS (Central Station)." The Dutch railway resisted only because it wanted to spare the costs that would arise if other cities also demanded a name change. Finally, the railway company gave in but stipulated that only the five largest Dutch railway stations (Amsterdam, Rotterdam, The Hague, Utrecht, and Leiden) could be designated as central stations. One of the victims of this policy was Almere's central station, which was renamed the Almere Center. Whether this caused any animosity between Almere and Leiden is unknown.

★ Leiden´s ode to Rembrandt

In autumn 2005, a sculpture called "Ode to Rembrandt" by the Dutch artist Jan Wolkers was installed at the Leiden train station. If the organizers had waited a few more months, the opening would have coincided with the 400th birthday of the greatest son of the city. However, Rembrandt van Rijn was not the only important figure born in Leiden, but also the sculpture Wolkers (1925-2007) himself. He actually organized the event to occur on his 80th birthday.

Glass was normally Wolkers's favorite material, but since some of his sculptures installed in public places were victims of vandalism, he insisted on a steel sculpture with glass elements placed at an unreachable height for "Ode to Rembrandt." The colorful shards in the windows of the sculpture are meant to refer to the colorful paintings of Rembrandt.

Rotterdam Blaak and its nickname

In 1982, the Rotterdam Blaak Railway Station got a subway connection. The subway was designed so that space was available to lay the elevated train station track itself under the earth later. The underground Blaak train station was opened in September 1993. So that one could find the station, a distinct modern above-ground access building was erected. The building soon got several nicknames by the population, including Fluitketel (flute kettle), Pedaalemmer (garbage bin), and putdeksel (manhole cover).

Rotterdam-Blaak station

Rotterdam´s Exit

In May 2006, the large letters "EXIT" hung above the entrance to the Rotterdam Central Station. That was not an error, but rather an art project, with which the city said goodbye to the old train station, a rather brutalist post-war construction. The station building from 1957 was then demolished to make way for a new building sufficient for modern requirements. The spectacular architecture of the new Rotterdam train station quickly got a nickname. The locals call the station "potato sack (Patatzak)."

Poster showing new Rotterdam central station

Utrecht Central Station

With approximately 150,000 passengers per day, Utrecht is the main transportation hub of the Dutch railway system. The headquarters of the Dutch railway company NS is located in Utrecht, and the Utrecht train station has the function of a zero point of the railway network of the Netherlands. At many stations in the country, a kilometer number is highlighted, indicating the track distance from Utrecht. Back in 1843, Utrecht already had its first station. However, this was soon designated as too small, and in 1855, a new building was erected. The central location of Utrecht was the reason why traffic grew quickly, and in 1865, there was again a renovation. This iteration lasted until 1936 when a new station was built. However, this then-new building would only last two years, when, in December 1938, it burned down to the ground. In 1939, a bright, elegant new building emerged from the ashes. The ridge of the roof of the station was appropriately decorated with the figure of a phoenix. However, this gleaming bird was demolished in the 1970s and replaced by an elevated shopping centre passage called the Hoog Catherijn. People commonly referred to the new centre as "Hoog Chagrijn (great sorrow)." A new station, which is rather unpopular among railway enthusiasts, was built in 2015. In the miniature park of Madurodam in the Hague, one can find a model of the new station. Additionally, there is also a replica the old building.

Utrecht Maliebaan

The strong growth in traffic at the Utrecht Central Station has led to frequent extensions and rebuilding work and its current faceless appearance. However, due to low traffic volumes, the Utrecht-Maliebaan station´s beauty has been preserved. Built in 1874, the station was decommissioned in 1939 for passenger traffic. In 1954, the Dutch railway museum was set up in the station. When they demolished the old central station of The Hague in the early 1970s, the royal waiting room was transported to Utrecht and rebuilt in the Maliebaan station. Since 2005, trains stop at Maliebaan station again, so that visitors to the railway museum, as it should be, can reach it by train.

Utrecht Maliebaan

Den Haag Centraal and Sjoelbak (shuffleboard)

The Den Haag Centraal Station was opened in 1973. It looks like a concrete block with sober dreary windows and is considered one of the ugliest train stations in the country. Since it is a terminal station (the second station of The Hague, Hollands Spoor, is a station with through traffic), it has the nickname Sjoelbak (shuffleboard). Sjoelen is a Dutch game, in which wooden discs must be maneuvered in four holes. The blunt-ended tracks of the station remind the Dutch of the wooden shuffleboard (Sjoelbak) of the game.

Utrecht Overecht and the slide

Utrecht Overdrecht station is the only station in Europe (and in the world) that can be reached via a children's slide. Instead of using stairs, you can slide down to the passage leading to the platforms. However, it is children rather than commuters who take advantage of this opportunity (officially called a 'transfer accelerator').

Slide in the station of Utrecht Overecht

★ Vleuten and the crafty mayor

Vleuten is a small station west of Utrecht on the way to The Hague. In 1930, the station was to be closed due to dwindling demand. To avoid a shutdown, the cunning mayor Verder decided to have unemployed people travel each day back and forth by train from Utrecht to Vleuten to increase ridership. Only in 2007 was the station closed, however, this was because a new modern station was built.

Bodegraven and the announcement

Located on the route Leiden-Utrecht, Bodegraven station (built in 1913) is a typical two-track through station with a platform on the left side of the track and a second one on the right side of the track. Therefore, the passengers were more surprised when one day, the announcement came that the train would enter on track three.

Gouda and the cheese

The Dutch city of Gouda is famous for its cheese. Somehow, the curves of the station roof are also reminiscent of cheese loaves. Among several of the arches are sculptures, however, none relating to the railways. One arch shows a few modes of transport though: a horse-drawn vehicle, a ship, and a man carrying a loaf of cheese.

Gouda station

Zaandam and the strange hotel

Zaandam is part of the Amsterdam metropolitan area and has already, in many aspects, been a trendsetter. Zaanstreek, a region along the Zaan river, was one of the earliest industrialized areas in Europe. Thousands of windmills located in the region provided the manufacturing industry of Amsterdam with energy. The Russian Tsar Peter the Great studied the art of shipbuilding in Zaandam. In 1971, the first McDonald's in Europe opened in Zaandam. Today, Zaandam's train station demonstrates that it belongs to the architectural avant-garde; the typical regional architecture, green dashed wooden facades, is satirized in a hotel construction, in which these traditional houses are seemingly stacked on top of each other. Additionally, the station building itself is realized in a toy style that is congruent with the surroundings.

Zaandam station

2.2 The other regions of the Netherlands

S-Hertogenbosch

A railway station similarly magnificent as Amsterdam once stood in `S-Hertogenbosch. Therefore, it is no surprise that the same architect was responsible for both buildings. However, during the Second World War, the station was damaged so badly that it was rebuilt in a modern form. Only two historic, 450-meter-long platform roofs from the pre-war railway station were retained. They bear witness to one of the largest railway architecture losses of the war.

Station ´S-Hertogenbosch

Valkenburg - the oldest

The station building in Valkenburg, opened on 23 October 1853, is the oldest still operating train station of the Netherlands. The architectural model for the building was the palace of the Dutch King Willem II in Tilburg. The station was built of marl, which is common in the area (the marl caves of Valkenburg are now a tourist attraction). ☞ In the past, people attempted to improve the acidic soil of dry marshes with the addition of marl. Since marl is not a fertilizer, but was initially confused with one, the fields soon leached out when proper fertilizer was not added. This led to the creation of the German term "ausmergeln (to exhaust the soil)."

★ Hulshorst

When a railway line was built from Utrecht to Zwolle in 1863, local property owners in the area Hulshorst gave over their land, yet only on the condition that trains would always stop there. Today, these landowners would probably turn in their grave because, contrary to the agreement, trains have not stopped in Hulshorst since 1987. Because of its remote location in a forest area, the station has always experienced low traffic numbers. The eminent Dutch poet Gerrit Achterberg (1905-1962) got out here when he visited his mistress. In a poem, which hangs on the facade of the building - used as a residential building today - he wrote the following about the station Hulshorst: "[It is] where the railroad running to the north comes to a pathetic creaking halt and nobody gets in and nobody gets out."

Lelystad station

The reclamation of the former Zuiderzee Flevoland created a 12th Dutch province. In 1986, Lelystad became the capital of the new province (named after Minister Cornelis Lely, who had advocated for the reclamation of the Zuiderzee). In 1988, the modern station Lelystad center was opened, with tracks connecting Lelystad to Amsterdam. The railway station has a covered glass hall with an island platform with two tracks. Outside the hall is space for another platform with two tracks. Corresponding viaducts were built to create the possibility of a later extension of a long rail line north to Groningen. However, this extension was not realized until December 2012 (since the corresponding passenger potential was not achieved), and the already-built iron railway viaducts at the station served the bicycle traffic for a long time.

Groningen´s cathedral of the winged wheel

Built in 1896 by Amsterdam architect Isaac Gosschalk, the station building of Groningen is one of the most beautiful in the Netherlands. When the station was restored in 1999, a ceiling, which was suspended in the 1960s into the concourse, was removed. The magnificent halls came to the fore again with the beautiful ceiling of the original with its round cupola. Due to the formal architecture and the winged wheel on the pediment of the Groningen train station, it has the nickname the cathedral of the winged wheel in Dutch (Cathedraal van het gevleugelde wiel). At the station square, another special thing is present: a white horse from the sculptor Jan de Baat. That "Peerd van Ome Loeks (the horse of Uncle Luke)" is a figure of a student song and is a symbol of Groningen.

Nijmegen (Nijmegen)

Except in the greater Rotterdam area, only a few Dutch stations were destroyed in the Second World War. An exception is Nijmegen. In February of 1944, British and American bombers were traveling towards their destination: Germany. However, bad weather forced them to turn back. As they flew over what they believed to be the Lower Rhine town of Goch, they dropped their bomb load. However, below them was the railway station district of Nijmegen. The bombs destroyed the station and killed 600.

Tilburg Kroepoekdak

Tilburg station was destroyed in the Second World War. A distinctive clock tower at the station serves as a reminder to those fallen in the war. Locals call the tower "Clothespin (Wasknijper)" due to its appearance. Also, the distinctive zigzag roof of the station building, which was designed in

1957 and opened in 1965, received a nickname. Tilburgers call it "Kroepeokdak (Indonesian crab chips)," which are also called prawn crackers in Holland.

Breda´s humble station

Breda, located in the province of Brabant in the south of the country, was a fortress city for a long time because of its proximity to the border. In the early days of the railroad era, the statutes of a fortress city required station buildings that could be quickly dismantled in the event of war. Therefore, a modest wooden station was built in Breda in 1855. Also, in 1863, a new building was built of wood. The humble station was ironically called "the business card of Breda." When Queen Wilhelmina paid a visit to Breda in 1894, the town's citizens quickly placed a stone wall in front of the station to camouflage it and spare them embarrassment because of its modest appearance. The town had to wait until 1968 to receive a modern station.

★ Eindhoven - the station as a radio

Eindhoven is also called the City of Light because, in 1891, Gerhard Philips founded here a factory for electric bulbs. From this factory, the technology giant Philips developed in the following decades. A large proportion of this expansion and success was thanks to the commercial canniness of Gerhard's brother Anton Philips (1874-1951). In a televised vote in 2004, he was chosen as one of the greatest Dutch. In front of the Eindhoven train station is a bronze statue of the pioneer. A centre of technology, Eindhoven (apart from Philips, the car manufacturer DAF was also present in the city) had to produce for the German war machine during World War II, and was, therefore, bombed into the ground by the Allies. By the way, Philips was able to save hundreds of Jews, who were declared as essential workers for the production. After the war, the railway station had to be rebuilt. As a tribute to the most important company of the city, the facade of the building was designed in the style of a Philips radio of the 1950s. To see the design, one must picture the clock as the adjuster, the station tower as an antenna, and the balcony façade as a resonance chamber.

Eindhoven station

Boxtel

Boxtel is a small railway station in the south of the Netherlands. As the number of tracks of the route Eindhoven was doubled from two to four, the old train station was demolished and replaced by a smaller modern construction. However, many passengers were already dissatisfied with the lack of services already present in the old station building. The following anecdote is told:

A customer came to the ticket counter and asked for a coffee. The railway employee replied, "You cannot get coffee from me; there's only coffee from the machines." The customer reflected for a moment and then responded, "if that is so, then I take tea."

2.3 Belgium

★ Antwerp - The Railway Cathedral

★ At the end of the 19th Century, the resource wealth of the Belgian Congo, whose inhabitants were brutally exploited, swept a lot of money into the pockets of the Belgian King Leopold II. In Brussels, he built boulevards and the triumph arch; in Antwerp, he built a large terminal station as a monument to himself. As a model for the new station, the king recommended to his architect the Lucerne train station, whose dramatic high dome had impressed him during stays in Switzerland. Another model for the station was the Pantheon in Rome. Eventually, the station opened in 1905. Due to its architecture and atmosphere, the station became known as a "railway cathedral." The British writer G.K. Chesterton once wrote about the similarities of stations and churches that:

"You will find a railway station in much of the quietude and consolation of a cathedral. It has many of the characteristics of a grand ecclesiastical building; it has vast arches, void spaces, colored lights, and above all, it has recurrence of ritual. It is dedicated to the celebration of water and fire: the two prime elements of human ceremonial."

At the opening of the station in 1905, King Leopold was surprised by its size. He stated ironically, "C'est une belle petite gare (That's a nice little station)." Later, the impressive railway station served as the backdrop for many films - partly standing in as the Brussels station, - which brought actors like Yves Montand, Michel Piccoli, and Charlotte Rampling into the station.

Antwerp and the conversion

The Antwerp train station was not destroyed in World War

II, but in the 1950s, the Vinalmont limestone dome of the station became porous. In 1953, bricks fell from the crown of the dome onto the station roof. In 1957, the skull of a passenger was fractured when he was hit by a falling stone. Protruding stones were anchored again, and the dome stones were jointed with a binding agent. Nevertheless, in the 1960s, there were plans for demolition of the station. In the 1970s, however, there was a change in thinking, and in 1975, the station was placed under the protection of historical monuments. In 1993, the renovation and rebuilding began with new underground levels. Since 2007, many trains no longer terminate at the station. In September 2009, the new station was then officially opened. The new station has four levels, which are connected by 48 escalators and 40 elevators. Security measures have taken be taken very seriously at the station. There are 275 fire detectors and 23 water pumps in the station. In the public area of the station, there are 199 surveillance cameras and 90 more in the tunnels. All the increased security measures provided no help when a cockatoo escaped the nearby Zoo of Antwerp in August 2009. The cockatoo settled in the iron structure of the platform hall roofs and could only be lured into a birdcage with food.

Exterior view of Antwerp CS

Brussels-Central/Centraal

Even before World War II, there were plans to connect the two Brussels terminal railway stations, the North and the South Station, via a tunnel and to build a new central station in between. The Art Nouveau architect Victor Horta was commissioned with designing the station building. However, the project was delayed during the Second World War, and the station was only finished in 1949, two years after Horta's death. The Central Station is, with 140,000 passengers per day - ahead of Brussels South (45,000) and Ghent (44 000) - the Belgian train station with the greatest number of passengers. Since traffic continues to grow and the station only three platforms, these had to be extended, creating more escalators and exits to cope with the huge flows of people. The entrance area has nine vertical windows with flag poles that stand for the then nine provinces of Belgium (with the division of Brabant into a Walloon and a Flemish part, there are, however, ten today). During the World Expo 1958 (at that time, the new signature Atomium building with its nine iron atoms symbolized the nine provinces as well), the Central Station was connected to the airport, and one could even at the station check-in directly at a Sabena terminal.

Station Brussels Central

★ Brussels-Luxembourg

The Brussels-Luxembourg station is situated so near to the site of the European Parliament in Brussels that the tracks were covered to create an above ground-level access to the Parliament. Trains run from this station via Luxembourg, where the Parliament's Secretariat is located, to Strasbourg, the main seat of Parliament. The former reception building of the station received an information center of the Parliament. As a replacement for the old station building, a new access was created. This was inaugurated in early 2009. On the wall of the entry tunnel, there is a reproduction of a drawing by the author of comics Georges Remi (1907-1983). Remi became world-famous under his pseudonym Hergé starting with an advertising campaign he created for the department store Innovation. Attached to the comic drawings are information boards mounted in four languages. The English version informs under the heading *Hergé pulls into the station Brussels-Luxembourg*: "In October 1932, Hergé, the creator of the famous *Adventures of Tintin*, staged a fun and delicious presentation for the good-natured people of Brussels...Glorious years, the triumph of the Belgian railways, and architecture that glorifies steel: this scene, which is remarkable in its pictorial development, provides us with valuable evidence of an epoch that is not too distant, but so different due to its clothing, its uniforms, and its strange machines."

Next to the picture is Hergé's signature. Such a "tag" is respected by Graffito artists. Hergé was born in Etterbeek, a community that is adjacent to the Luxembourg station (the relatively narrowly defined Brussels region consists of 19 municipalities). The next stop is therefore: Etterbeek.

Brussels Airport Station

Since it is close to the railway line from Brussels to Liège and due to the 1958 World Expo, Brussels had the world's first direct railway connection to an airport. In May 1955, then young Belgian King Baudouin opened the airport station. From the airport, there was also a helicopter shuttle service to the city. Originally, the trains heading to the Central Station left on a special track. Later, however, the trains connected the airport to Brussels Midi Station, where high-speed trains to London and Paris departed beginning in the 1990s. At the end of 1994, a new terminal was opened, and a new airport station was built. In 2005, a line connecting the railway with Liège was built. Since then, one can go directly by train from Leuven to the airport. In 2012, a connection to Antwerp has was added. This project is called the "Diabolo," because the airport, like in a juggling diabolo toy, hangs at the end of a rail line triangle.

Until a few years ago, the airport in the Brussels suburb of Zaventem was called Nationaal Brussel/Bruxelles-National. This confused some people because it was actually an international airport. Germans are responsible for the airport's location. During World War II, the German military, as occupiers, dug out the first runways (in World War I, the first Zeppelin landing place was at Haren, the current NATO headquarters, was also created by the Germans). Today, a joke is told about how this site was chosen. When the Germans asked locals where would be a good location to put an airport, they pointed in the direction of Zaventem because it was often foggy there.

Brussels Jazz Station

In the Brussels district of Saint-Josse-ten-Noode, there is a jazz club called Jazz Station. The name is not far-fetched because the locality uses the facilities of a closed down train station, which was originally built in 1885. Below the Jazz Station, trains continue to pass through (they link the European quarter with the Gare du Nord). Stairs lead down to the tracks, but the platforms, overgrown with grass, cannot be reached anymore.

Former Saint Josse station (Today, Jazz Station)

Brussels Midi

Bruxelles Midi is the South Station of the Belgian capital. Once there were South and North railway station terminus stations but, when they were connected by a tunnel in the 1950s, they became through traffic railway stations. Additionally, the station in the town center became Bruxelles Central in 1949. A German tourist, with not-so-perfect French, was surprised that the Midi station was on the southern edge of the city center. He had confused the word "midi" (it means midday/south) as "Mitte" (German for middle, center).

★ Brussels Watermael and Paul Delvaux

Belgium has produced several significant surrealist painters, including René Magritte and Paul Delvaux (1897-1994). Typical images of Delvaux show pale naked women in the foreground. The background often shows realistic land-scapes, sceneries, and often railways. On several images also appears the train station of the Brussels municipality of Watermael because Delvaux lived near the station for a long time and used it for rides to the city center. A few years ago, a Belgian artist rented at the station and used it as his studio.

Brussels Schaerbeek and the hostel

The Flemish neo-renaissance-style station building of the Brussels municipality of Schaerbeek, built in 1913, has been converted into a railway museum (Train World). The museum was originally planned to open in 2010 to mark the 175th anniversary of the railway in Belgium but finally opened in 2014. Not far from the railway station, a hostel is under construction, which is typically Belgian quirky and should appeal to the taste of railway enthusiasts. A railway sleeping car was placed on the roof of the train hostel in October 2013. Since the opening in 2014, it is possible to stay in a sleeping car compartment with a view over the rooftops of Brussels.

Schaerbeek- the sleeping car on the roof of the hostel

Mechelen and the milliaire column

On 5 May 1835, (half a year before the opening of the first German railway line between Nuremberg and Fürth) the first passenger train on the European mainland left Mechelen. A proper station was not yet available in the city. However, Mechelen already had a zero stone from which the distances in the Belgian railway network were measured. Normally, such a milestone should be kept in the same place, yet the column, which serves as a zero point, was moved over multiple times. For example, the column moved when the beautiful train station from 1888 - with its impressive platform hall - was demolished between 1958 and 1960 and replaced by an unspeakably faceless building. The Brussels World Expo of 1958 led to a modernization of thinking and inspired the demolition plans. Today, the distance column called "miliaire/mijlpaal (mileage)" is already sitting at its seventh different position: in the middle of a roundabout in front of the train station. The first location of the "miliaire" is marked by a round base in the main hall of the station.

Miliaire Column in front of Mechelen station

Mechelen-Nekkerspoel

In 1997, the station building of the station Mechelen-Nekkerspoel was sold to a media company. After that, the brick stone building from 1903 was adorned with the poster saying, "Ceci n'est pas une gare (this is not a train station)." This inscription was inspired by a picture of the Belgian surrealist René Magritte (1898-1962) showing a tobacco pipe with the inscription, "Ceci n'est pas une pipe (this is not a pipe)." In 2009, the railway company bought back the train station building. Now it should really be called, "Ceci n'est pas un bureau (this is not an office)."

The inverted station of Ronse

In 1844 in the Flemish city of Bruges once one of the first train stations on the European continent was opened. But the station was too close to the city center and only three decades later, it suffered from a lack of space. Therefore, it was decided to build a new station further out. The town Ronse (Renaix in French) on the Dutch/French language border also needed a new station, because there was so far only a modest station hut. So it was decided in Ronse, to demolish the station of Bruges, stone by stone and rebuild in Ronse. When the building opened in 1881, it was noticed however, that the station had been built the wrong way round. But this was not a big problem, because the side towards the tracks is almost identical with the city side.

Ronse Station

45

Halle (Flanders)

In 1995, the neo-Flemish renaissance style brick station of Halle, 20 km south of Brussels, had to make way for a high-speed line. The municipality reassured citizens that the station building would be rebuilt with its original elements elsewhere to serve as a cultural centre. However, concerned citizens later found out that the parts of the building were not stored carefully, but carelessly dumped in a meadow on the edge of a garbage dump.

Verviers

The completion of the monumental railway station of Verviers was delayed because of WWI and the economic crisis of the 1920s. When the station finally opened in 1930, its architecture was not quite contemporary anymore. On the wall of the ticket hall, works of the sculptor Joseph Gérard (1873-1946) can be seen, including the Lafontaine fable of the tortoise and the hare, implemented as an allegory of traveling by train.

☞ A stampede scene in the disaster movie *The Cloud* (*Die Wolke* in German, 2006) was shot in Verviers station because the film crew could not gain permission to shoot the scene in the German station of Bad Hersfeld or any other DB-station.

Leuven and the bikes

The Belgian university town of Leuven has 100,000 inhabitants and about 30,000 are students. Many students commute daily by train and ride a bike into town. Therefore, more bikes are parked at this station than in no other European city outside of the Netherlands. A huge bicycle parking garage east of the station has 4,000 parking places. Only at the very end of the garage, far away from the entrance, does the bicycle density decrease. However, due to an increasing number of students, it is also likely that these places soon will be occupied.

In the coming years, the Ghent station will become an even bigger bike station (10,000 places). The intention is to provide adequate long-term storage capacity because the current 2,000 installed bike parking areas around the station are no longer sufficient.

The leaning tower of Ghent

In 1913, there was a world exhibition in Ghent, and on this occasion, the St. Pieters train station was built in a strange, vaguely oriental fantasy style. Over the years, the slender clock tower of the station increasingly tilted and thus became the "Leaning Tower of Ghent" (30 cm tilt). In 2006, for security reasons, it was eventually knocked down and rebuilt with a solid concrete core and a brick façade.

Gent St. Pieters and the once leaning station tower

Liège, the station in quotation marks

Liège was one of the first cities on the continent with a train station. In 1842, the first station building was inaugurated in

47

this city. For the World Expo in 1958, the building was replaced by a modern building in the 1950s style. This building did not age with dignity and already looked pretty bad in the 1980s. Therefore, it was decided in the 1990s - in the wake of the high-speed route Brussels-Cologne - to rebuild the station a short distance from the old location. The Spanish architect Santiago Calatrava won the commission with a bold design, which provided a huge train station roof (200 m long, 35 m high). In 2000, the construction began. However, it was nearly ten years later, only on 18 September 2009, that it could be inaugurated. During the long construction period, the population mockingly called the train station - officially known as Liège-Guillemins - "Liège-Guillemets (Liège in quotation marks)."

Liège-Guillemins

Mons-Snow
The construction of the spectacular station in Liège (Liège-Guillemins) gave the city leaders of Mons the idea of replacing their unrepresentative 1950s station with a spectacular new building as well. Once again, the Spanish architect Calatrava won, and as in Liège, the planned station shines in white. The old station was demolished in the

48

summer of 2013. At that time, upside down suspended station signs could be seen on the platforms. Instead of MONS, you could now read SNOW, which almost seemed like a reference to the future snow-white station. After a bad start, the completion of the project is years behind schedule, and it is now hoped that it will finally open at the end of 2020.

Binche and the ticketing

The Walloon city of Binche has a nice station, built between 1905-1910 in the neo-gothic style of Brabant. Binche is considered an important carnival town. The historic Carnival parade with its ostrich feather-adorned "Gilles," clown-like performers who throw oranges, is included in UNESCO's World Cultural Heritage list for "Masterpieces of the Oral and Intangible Heritage of Humanity."

Yet, the Carnival is not the only trait that Binche has in common with the Rhineland. Above the ticket counters of the station, which lies in the French-speaking part of Belgium, one can read the German word "Fahrkartenverkauf (Ticket Sales)." Today, nobody knows anymore why this is the case.

Binche Station

Charleroi Sud and the melody

The city of Charleroi in Belgium does not have the best reputation. It is considered a dirty, heavy industry city and a hotbed of crime, run by corrupt politicians. Its nickname is, therefore, "Chicago on the Sambre." Bad transport planning led to the construction of a subterranean metro (Métro Léger de Charleroi), which is underutilized, and has oversized, rarely used subway stations. Branch lines were opened, never used, and now are rotting.

Nevertheless, people of the city maintain a certain local pride. On the platforms, announcements are preceded by the first notes of the folk hymn "Pays de Charleroi (Charleroi country)." The song has the following refrain: *Pays de Charleroi, C'est toi que je préfère Le plus beau coin de terre (Charleroi country, you're the region, which I prefer, the nicest place on earth).*

The rest of Belgium shakes its collective head in response.

★ Marbehan and Maurice Grevisse

Belgian students commuting by train from Marbehan in the Ardennes to Arlon in southern Belgium are reminded of the rules of French grammar at the station. From a window of Marbehan station, there is a portrait of the Belgian grammarian Maurice Grevisse (1895-1980), who was born in Rulles, not far from Marbehan. Grevisse wrote *Le Bon Usage*, a grammar book on the French language, which is now a highly regarded standard work that is normally called "Le Grevisse." In the absence of a famous inhabitant, Marbehan refers to the well-known grammarian from the neighbouring village.

3. France

3. 1 Paris and Northern France

Paris Gare du Nord

With 500,000 passengers per day, Paris Nord (North) is - including the suburban RER-system - the largest railway station in Europe. Yet, that was not always the case. The first North Station opened in 1846 and was still relatively small. However, with increasing traffic to Holland and Belgium, it ran into capacity problems within a few years. This should soon become obvious, as the following anecdote shows. In 1855, Britain's Queen Victoria traveled by train, ferry, and again by train from Lille to visit the World Expo that took in Paris. On the platform of the North station, a welcoming committee of French dignitaries anxiously awaited the Queen's arrival. The reception should have been perfect, and everywhere at the station, "Welcome" slogans hung. Yet, as the train entered the station, it slowed down and suddenly stopped. The minutes passed, and finally, the train moved again, but to the dismay of those waiting, in the opposite direction. Finally, an explanation came: there was no room in the station for the royal train. Therefore, it had to be diverted to the more spacious Gare de l'Est. With great haste, the reception decorations were removed, and the reception committee travelled to the (not very distant) Eastern Station compound, where the train with the queen just arrived. After that event, it was decided to enlarge the North Station within two years to three times its original size. On its façade, eight statues of women represent major destinations in the North and East, including Brussels, Amsterdam, London, Vienna, Berlin, Warsaw, Cologne, and Frankfurt. However, from Gare du Nord, there were never trains to Frankfurt or Vienna.

Lille Flandres

When the Paris North Station was rebuilt around 1860 in a more representative way, the old façade was taken down, transported by train to Lille, and re-assembled there. The citizens of Lille were initially not particularly enthusiastic by the idea of a Paris train station being recycled in their city. Later, an additional floor and a clock tower were added. Nevertheless, the ground floor of the Lille Flandres station still shows how the Paris Gare du Nord station looked before 1860.

With the opening of the Channel Tunnel, Lille got a second station for the high-speed traffic called "Lille Europe," with L-shaped office buildings next to it. Inside the premises, it is rather windy. Therefore, the station got the nickname "Gare aux courants d'air (Station of Drafts)."

Paris Gare d'Austerlitz

When Paris was besieged by German troops in 1870 and 1871, the Parisians used the high hall of the Austerlitz train station to produce Montgolfier balloons. With the help of the balloons, pigeons, messages, and a politician were transported through enemy lines.

Paris Gare de Lyon

The Gare de Lyon in Paris was built for the Universal World Exhibition in 1900. There are two remarkable things about the station: the clock tower, reminiscent of the Big Ben Tower of the UK Parliament in London, and the splendid restaurant Le Train Bleu, which once had a buffet for exhausted travelers, but now houses upscale gastronomy in a Second Empire setting with stucco and finely worked ceiling frescoes. Train Bleu is named after the luxury trains that once departed from here to the south of France.

Paris Saint-Lazare

With 27 tracks and more than a quarter of a million passengers per day, Paris Saint-Lazare is one of the largest railway stations in France. For art lovers, it is a particularly intriguing station. In 1877, the impressionistic painter Claude Monet captured the smoke of the steam engines in a painting of Saint-Lazare station. In 2008, the station was seriously plagued by rats. Work on the underground water-supply of the building had driven the rodents into daylight.

The pinball machine in the centre of Paris

In 1976, the former market halls of Paris were demolished and replaced by a futuristic shopping center with an underground RER-station. However, the new complex *Chatelet les Halles* was controversial from the start. The architecture did not harmonize well with the neighboring church of Saint Eustache, and the glass and plastic facades did not age with dignity. Additionally, the flow of passengers through the underground mass transit station was not optimal. In the station, massive columns that restrict the view but are not structurally necessary make orientation difficult. Due to its disorienting nature, it received the nickname "flipper" since, like a ball in a pinball machine, the passengers crr back and forth here. Meanwhile, the complex has been renovated. It which is, by the way, with 750,000 visitors per day, one of the busiest train stations in France.

Deauville and the model

In 1931, a new station opened in the seaside resort of Deauville in Normandy, its design mirroring the regional style of Norman architecture. Today, the station is called Gare de Trouville-Deauville. The station building has a half-timbered facade and three-pointed gables. Supposedly, many different stations built overseas by the French in colonial times are copies of Deauville, including Da Lat in Vietnam and Pointe Noire in the Congo. However, these stations do not truly resemble their supposed model.

★ Rouen and the Belgian poet

On the right bank of the Seine River, the so-called Right Bank main station of Rouen has one of the most beautiful station halls in France. It was constructed in 1912-24 by the architect Adolphe Dervaux in the Art Nouveau style and inaugurated by the French president in 1928. Before construction had finished, a disaster occurred in the station. The Belgian poet Emile Verhaeren was at a conference in France in November 1916. He had already produced pacifistic poems against the ravages of World War I. Now he was trying to strengthen the friendship between Britain, France, and Belgium. Upon arrival, Verhaeren was received at the station by an enthusiastic crowd. However, the crowd pushed him onto the tracks, and the train rolled over him. The French government wanted a grave in the Pantheon in Paris in his honor, but his family insisted on a funeral in a Belgian military cemetery.

Cherbourg's large station

When it was opened in 1933 after five years of construction, the Art Deco-styled Cherbourg Gare Maritime building was the second-largest in France after the Palace of Versailles. The station concourse is 240 meters long, and the station complex is 93 meters wide. This station covered an area of more than two hectares. The clock tower of the station was 67 meters tall and had a nautical function. Cherbourg, at the northern end of the Norman-Contentin peninsula, was then an important international port, even for passengers. The station had been so generously dimensioned to absorb passengers from giant ocean liners on one side and the incoming of passenger trains from Paris St Lazare on the other side. During the Second World War, the military traffic brought intensive use of station facilities. However, the station was also hit by bombs, and the clock tower destroyed. The tower was not rebuilt because of the development of air transport, which brought with it a decline of transatlantic shipping traffic. Soon after, the station became a kind of dinosaur. In the years between 1999 and 2002, the station was rebuilt into the maritime museum *Cité de la Mer*.

The sugar beet station

In France, railway traffic is often oriented towards maximum speed (and seen from Paris), not necessarily towards connecting city centres. It so happens that sometimes new high-speed stops in medium-sized cities are far from the city center with limited local transport connections. An example of this phenomenon is the Haute Picardie TGV station on a green field site between Amiens and Saint-Quentin. Its nickname is "*gare de betteraves* (sugar beet station)."

Lusigny and the model train station

Lusigny-sur-Base is a village in the region of Champagne-Ardenne (1650 inhabitants) in eastern France. Since the 1990s, trains do not stop at Lusigny anymore. Nevertheless, due to its appearance, it is one of the most famous train stations in France. The reason is that a miniature copy of the station in HO format was for many decades one of the hits sales of the French model train manufacturer *Jouef*, and model train fans of all generations have grown up with it.

3.2 Alsace and Lorraine

Metz - the strategic military station

The railway station of Metz was built from 1905 to 1908 for military strategic reasons. Lorraine belonged to Germany at that time, and the new station allowed a connection to the so-called "Kanonenbahn (Cannon Railway)" to Berlin. The platforms were very long and very broad so that horses in the war could be quickly loaded and unloaded. The station was designed to make it possible to transport an army within 24 hours to Lorraine. However, the unfavorable terrain required the building to be grounded on 3000 reinforced concrete piles. The architectural style was neo-Romanesque, which was regarded as particularly German. Kaiser Wilhelm II took a personal interest in every detail of the design of the station, as he did in transforming the city's cathedral, and asked for changes in the plans of architect Jürgen Kröger.

Colmar and the similarity

A few years ago, the French railway magazine *La Vie du Rail* reported that the Colmar station, which was built between 1905 and 1907, looked very similar to Gdansk railway station (the station's tower mimics Gdansk's city hall tower), which was built from 1894 to 1900. One reader pointed out that the similarity should be no surprise considering that, at the time of their constructions, both stations were built in the same country: Germany.

Strasbourg - the legacy of the Germans

In 1883, the first Orient Express ran from Paris to Vienna. The train stopped in the new Strasbourg Central Station, which opened the same year, and which had magnificent rooms for the German Kaiser, since the city became a part of

Germany in 1871. Twenty years earlier, swing bridges had been built into the railway bridge over the Rhine to stave off the enemy in the event of war (rather to take the path, because a swing bridge that has probably been turned away does not really block the enemy). The Strasbourgers never warmed up to the Wilhelmine style station design with its somewhat bland sandstone facade. That explains why, in 2006, a spectacular glass hull was attached to the station. Along with the newly laid out lawn, this results in a surreal appearance of the railway square.

Strasbourg station

Mulhouse

The architecture of the station of Mulhouse is purely French. The first two stations were built in the 1840s, and the third, still existing station, was built from 1928 to 1932. In the period between 2006 and 2009, the station square was rebuilt to make space for the newly built tram-train system.

3.3 Rest of France and Monaco

★ Perpignan - the spiritual center of the world

The Spanish painter Salvador Dali (1904-1989) was often traveling by train from his home in northern Spain to Paris. The railway line ran through the Perpignan train station, and Dali always felt that this station of stirred up inspiration within him. Therefore, he saw the station as a spiritual center of Western metaphysics and even as a mystical and cosmic center of the universe. In 1965, Dali even donated a picture to this station. The French railway was flattered and commissioned Dali to create six posters around the railway theme. Today, a figure representing Dali sits on the station roof to commemorate the painter.

★ St. Nazaire and the fall through the glass roof

Alan Eugene Magee, an American born in 1919, died in December 2003 at the age of 84. However, already more than 60 years earlier, it was almost a miracle that he was still alive. Magee was flying in a bomber plane over the French coastal town of St. Nazaire, when the plane was hit by German fire. The plane began a downward spin, and Magee - unable to find a functioning parachute - slipped out and lost conscience. Magee fell from 6400 meters up and finally struck through the glass roof of the station of St. Nazaire. Yet, surprisingly, he survived the fall. When he regained consciousness, he said, "I do not know how I am got here but thank God I'm alive." The Germans showed the pilot respect and nursed him as best they could (the others in the airplane were bailed out with parachutes). In 1993, 50 years after the incident, a monument was erected in the city for Magee and his flight crew. The historic railway station of Saint-Nazaire later declined rapidly, as did the city, which went downhill with the shipyard crisis. In 1955, a new building was constructed, and since then, it lies near the harbour. Its design integrates maritime elements and resembles the deck of a ship.

Limoges and the Tortoise

Limoges in southwest France has a dome-shaped concourse, in front of which a clock tower stands like a lighthouse. A traveler is said to have proclaimed when faced with its mosque-like appearance, "Are we in Constantinople already?" The station built by architect Roger Gonthier (1884-1978) opened in 1929 and was once described as a turtle who married a candle. The station design demonstrates the commercial tradition of Limoges as a porcelain city. The impressive glass dome was destroyed by fire in 1998, but later faithfully reconstructed.

★ Roanne and the absence of President

On 24 May 1920, at the station of Roanne (Loire department), a welcome committee was ready for the French President Paul Deschanel, who was supposed to arrive via the night train at 7 a.m. Yet, word got around that the president had mysteriously disappeared from the night train. Finally, they found the president in a car of the railway line signalman. What had happened? On the eve of train voyage, the president was leaning against the open window of his sleeping car. Somehow, he seemed to have lost his balance and fell off the train. Fortunately, the train was driving at a low speed through a construction site. The President was in his pajamas and stumbled bloodied along the tracks until he met with employees on a train, who brought him to the next cabin of the railway signalman. There he introduced himself as the President of France. The flagman was skeptical, but informed the police. The flagman's wife said later, "I immediately knew that this was a gentleman because he had clean feet."

Ardèche and the lack of station

The Ardèche department in the southern French region of Rhône-Alpes is a curiosity in terms of railways: it is the only one in France that does not have a train station.

La Ciotat - the first car movie

The Lumière brothers are considered the inventors of the cinema film. In 1895, they shot a one-minute film about the arrival of a train in the station of La Ciotat in Southern France. This was the first railroad film. When the film was shown, audiences were terrified because they thought the train would run them over.

Saint-Dalmas de Tende and the changing border

The Tenda railway line, with its spectacular scenery, connects Turin with the Mediterranean coast and runs on Italian and French territory. During the 20th century, the border moved back and forth along the central part of the line. In 1928, the Tenda region belonged to Italy, and Mussolini ordered a representative border station to be built in the village of Saint-Dalmas de Tende. In 1947, the town became French again. On the facade of the Italian style station building, the shadows of the former Italian railway station letters from Santo Dalmazzo di Tenda are still visible.

Marseille Saint-Charles and the stairs

Built in 1848 and renovated in 2006, the Marseille Saint-Charles terminus railway station is located on a small hill.

The terminus is linked to the low-lying city via a monumental staircase with 104 steps, which was built in 1926. The foot of the staircase is flanked by two sensual females statues of the sculptor Louis Botinelly (1883-1962), which represent the French colonies in Asia and Africa. In the book *Dictionnaire des Amoureux de Marseille*, author Paul Lombard, says that as a schoolboy, he and his cronies particularly appreciated the pronounced femininity of the statue which is supposed to represent the colonies in Africa.

The wrong Monaco

In April 2008, two Italian women traveled from Trieste to Munich to pick up their nephew, who was expected with the night train from Paris. However, the cousin was nowhere to see. An investigation by the police revealed that the cousin had landed in Monaco. After all, Munich is *Monaco di Baviera* in Italian, and the nephew asked for a ticket to Monaco at the station in Paris. The aunts decided to go by car to the Principality to pick him up.

4.Great Britain and Ireland

4.1 Greater London

London Euston and the modernization

London Euston was once a railway station in the neoclassical style, built in 1837. The entrance portal ("Euston Arch") had powerful, 22-meter-high pillars. However, to the regret of many, the Euston Arch was demolished and replaced by a banal modern building. The loss of this architectural gem resulted in the UK strengthening the protection of historic transport and manufacturing industry buildings, which were not considered as heritage before.

London St. Pancras

The St. Pancras station in London is a massive neo-Gothic building. It is characterized by two large structural features. The first is a large hotel, integrated into its façade, that has long stood empty, and has recently been redeveloped. The second special feature is the huge rail shed, covering all tracks; the first of this construction type. Since its re-opening as the terminal of the Eurostar Channel tunnel trains in November 2007, there is another record: the station has the longest champagne bar in Europe. Upon its opening, the press somewhat exaggerated the beauty of the train station. Since the track level is separated from the entrance and shopping level and Eurostar passengers have to go through security checks, the station does not offer the typical terminal experience with lined up trains in front of a passenger concourse. The atmosphere is rather sterile. The vaults, which now house shops, were formerly used for the storage of beer, which was transported from the countryside to the English capital.

St. Pancras and the graves

The St. Pancras Railway Station complex was partially built on cemetery grounds. Therefore, several of the deceased had to be reburied. Commissioned with the oversight of these activities was the church restorer and architect Thomas Hardy (1840-1928). Hardy later became one of the most important writers of England.

London King's Cross

In the film *Harry Potter And The Chamber Of Secrets,* scenes, like the ones where Harry, Hermione, and Ron were trying to catch the Hogwarts Express, were filmed in Kings Cross. For outdoor shooting, this film crew, however, chose the photogenic St. Pancras station on the other side of the street.

★ Liverpool Street Station

In front of the Liverpool Street Station, there is a memorial, created by the sculptor Frank Meisler (1929-2018), to the children's transport. Meisler himself and other Jewish children managed to escape in a cattle wagon from Gdansk via Berlin to Liverpool Street Station in August 1939.

London Waterloo and the Necropolis

Waterloo station (opened in 1848) in London covers the UK's largest railway compound. A few years later, a devastating cholera epidemic broke out in London. In 1854, next to the main station building, a Necropolis station was set up, from which a funeral procession train left each day to what was then the world's largest cemetery, the Brookwood Cemetery in Surrey. There were even separate platforms for deceased Anglicans and other faiths. In the Necropolis railway station, there was a bar with a sign, upon which the pun "spirits served here" was written. During the Second World War, the station fell victim to the bomb hail and was not rebuilt.

London Paddington and the three statues

London Paddington Station is a monument to books and friends. Agatha Christie´s novel *16:50 from Paddington Station* starts with a scene at this station. Additionally, the children's book character Paddington Bear is named after the station. A statue of the little bear can be found in the concourse. And yet, more statues can be seen in the station, including one of the great British railway and tunnel construction engineer Isambard Kingdom Brunel (1806-1859) and one for the First World War casualties among the employees working for the Great Western Railway.

London Vauxhall and dangerous relief

In July 2008, in the train station of Vauxhall, a 41-year-old Polish teacher died. He had travelled to Britain as a tourist to refresh his knowledge of English. In the station, there are no toilets, so the tourist ran to the end of the platform to relieve himself without other people noticing. However, one of the rails on which he urinated on was a power transmission rail with 750 volts (power rails are often used in the UK instead of catenary). The urine stream directed the electric flow into the body of the man, resulting in his death. By the way, the Russian word for "railway station (Vokzal)" is derived from the town of Vauxhall (see page 114).

★ Broad Street Station

In 1986, the Broad Street station in London, built in 1865, was demolished. A new station was not built since there was already a station directly next to it: the Liverpool station. Broad Street was once one of the busiest stations in London. In 1902, it had 27 million passengers, about 75,000 per day. However, by 1985, the daily passenger numbers dropped to 6,000, of which only 300 passengers arrived during the morning peak period. Between 1983 and 1984, a few years before the demolition of the station, the ex-Beatle Paul McCartney wrote and starred in the film *Give My Regards to Broad Street* (furthermore, an album with this title was produced by him). In one of the last scenes of the film, McCartney goes into the station and sits alone on a bench. In this film, the English actor Ralph Richardson had (1902-1983) his last appearance.

The following railway anecdote is told about Ralph Richardson. An old friend once saw Richardson in a London train station and exclaimed, "My dear Robertson," how have you changed? You look younger, your face is round, and you have a good colour. You have even shaved off your mustache." The Richardson stared dumbfounded at the man and said, "But my name is not Robertson." "Oh," said the man, "you've also changed the name."

Fenchurch Street Station

The tower located close to Fenchurch Street station has lent its name to several things. First, it is one of the stations which occur in the British standard issue of the game Monopoly. Second, the skater fashion brand *Fenchurch* is named after the station. The Fenchurch logo looks a bit like arches in a church, or as branching tracks. In Douglas Adams's book, *So Long, and Thanks for All the*

Fish - the fourth volume of his series *Hitchhiker's Guide to the Galaxy* - the female protagonist Fenchurch is named after the station because Adams supposedly got the idea for the character while at that station. Actually, he got the idea in Paddington station, but because there was already a Paddington Bear, he decided to name the protagonist after the Fenchurch station.

4.2 South and Southeast England

Box - the mysterious tunnel

In the county of Wiltshire in the west of England, there is the London-Bristol railway line near the village of Box the famous Box Tunnel. It is rumoured to have been laid out by the famous engineer Isambard Brunel so that the sun would shine through on the 9th April, his birthday. When the tunnel was dug, the engineers realised that the rock made good building material, and therefore, additional mines were set up for its degradation. The resulting caves were used by the government during the Second World War to store ammunition and for experiments with new weapons. An underground news center was established, with shafts that led to the support point located above the tunnel. Finally, there was a whole system of tunnels and caverns, some kind of underground city complete with platforms and courtyards for the train. During the Cold War, a nuclear bomb shelter was built here, as the site could easily be reached from London, with space for the government and the royal family in the event of a nuclear war.

★ Dartford and the accidental meeting

Mick Jagger and Keith Richards were born in 1943 in Dartford, Kent, and went to school there. Yet, after their school days, they lost touch with each other. Mick Jagger studied at the London School of Economics, and Keith Richards studied at Sidcup Art College. In October 1961, they bumped into each other at the Dartford train station. Both noted that they still had a great interest in music and decided to form a band: the Rolling Stones.

Slough and the dog in the display case

Slough, a city west of London, already had its first railway station in 1840. In 1842, Queen Victoria, on her first train ride from her royal castle in Windsor to London Paddington, boarded a train here. Since the principal of the elite Eton School near Windsor did not want a train station too close by, Slough was the closest train station to Windsor a long time.

Today, train station visitors are surprised to find a stuffed dog in a glass case on platform five. This is Jim, a dog that was used from 1894 until his death in 1896 to raise money for the widows and orphans fund of the Great Western Railway. After Jim's death, he was stuffed and placed in a glass case, which has a slot to donate money.

★ Reading and the lost manuscript

The British officer T.E. Lawrence (1888-1935, later known as Lawrence of Arabia) was travelling around Christmas time in 1919 from London to Oxford. At the Reading station, he had to change trains. When the train started to move, he noticed to his horror that he had forgotten his briefcase on the train platform. In his briefcase, there was the almost completed manuscript of his book *The Seven Pillars of Wisdom*, which reproduced his experiences in Arabia. Arriving at the station in Oxford, he had to call Reading station. However, the bag with the manuscript was not found. Since he had destroyed his notes earlier, he had no choice but to rewrite as many as 250,000 words from memory again.

★ Wolferton Royal Station

Among the many possessions of the British royal family is also an estate at Sandringham in the county of Norfolk near the North Sea coast in eastern England. Once, the village of Wolferton had the closest train station to the property, and therefore, there was a Royal Station here, where the royal train arrived. One day, however, an uninvited guest arrived at the railway station: the Russian monk Rasputin, who demanded to see the king. However, the king wanted to have nothing to do with the sinister monk, and he was promptly placed on the next train to London.

When King George VI. died in 1952, his body was transported to London by train from the royal railway station in Wolferton. In 1966, the railway line and the associated station were closed. The station became a museum in which one could admire the interiors of the royal trains, including Queen Victoria's travel bed. However, the museum was closed, and the station building is now a private residence and not accessible.

Portsmouth Harbour

Portsmouth Harbour is a train station, whose platforms reach down to the wharf. The location is considered a security risk, as car ferries run close to the tracks. Therefore, there are plans to move the train station away from the water's edge and towards inland. There is the following station joke:

An elderly lady asked the railway staff, "Does the train stop at Portsmouth Harbour?" He responded, "I hope so. Otherwise, there will be a big splash."

★ Dilton Marsh maintenance

The British railway poet Sir John Betjeman (1906-1984) once wrote the following poem about the maintenance station Dilton Marsh, which lies on the railway line from Salisbury to Westbury (Bath) in the West of England:

Was it worth keeping the Halt open,
We thought as we looked at the sky
Red through the spread of the cedar-tree,
With the evening train gone by?
Yes, we said, for in summer the anglers use it,
Two and sometimes three
Will bring their catches of rods and poles and perches
To Westbury, home for tea.
There isn't a porter. The platform is made of sleepers.
The guard of the last train puts out the light
And high over lorries and cattle the Halt unwinking
Waits through the Wiltshire night.
O housewife safe in the comprehensive churning
Of the Warminster launderette!
O husband down at the depot with car in car-park!
The Halt is waiting yet.
And when all the horrible roads are finally done for,
And there's no more petrol left in the world to burn,
Here to the Halt from Salisbury and from Bristol
Steam trains will return.

While the British Railways closed many small railway stops, the less frequented Dilton Marsh Halt survived, perhaps because it was immortalized in Betjeman's poem. The station was very underfunded. Earlier, there was not even a vending machine there. At the stop, a note was attached, which said, "Will passengers please obtain tickets from Mrs. H Roberts Holmdale, seventh house up the hill." In 1994, ten years after Betjeman's death, a decent platform

69

was finally created. Betjeman's daughter opened the new station, read the poem, and inaugurated a plaque with the text of the poem.

4.3 Middle- and Northern England

★ Preston and Wallace and Gromit

Nick Parker, the director of the famous Wallace and Gromit clay animation films, is from Preston in North West England (Lancashire). For a few years, there were plans to erect a Wallace & Gromit sculpture in the station. The railway company was positive about this plan. However, such a sculpture has not been realized. Yet, the station bar features a Wallace & Gromit picture on the wall.

Manchester Liverpool Road Station

The station building, which was reconstructed in 1830, is the oldest still-standing station building in the world. However, the station was also one of the earliest to be shut down. In 1844, the last passenger train left the station. Until 1975, the station was a depot for goods. Today, it houses a science museum.

Liverpool Edge Hill

Liverpool Edge Hill station, built in 1836, is the oldest station in the world still in use. However, today, the Lime Street train station is the most important one in Liverpool. Because of the gradient between Edge Hill and Lime Street, the locomotives in Edge Hill were originally disconnected. The cars travelled to Lime Street by gravity and with the help of brakes. For the return trip, the trains were aided by winches. Today, Edge Hill has only a few passengers and only a few trains due to its proximity to Lime Street. By the way, "Getting off at Edge Hill" is also a slang expression for *coitus interruptus* in English.

Huddersfield Station

During the 1800s, as the neo-Gothic style was also en vogue for train stations in the south of England, the north of the country tended to focus on neoclassical architecture. A good example of a neoclassical styled station is the one opened in 1847 in Huddersfield (6000 daily travelers). The entrance portal, which resembles a Greek temple, has six Corinthian columns. The poet John Betjeman described the facade of the building as the "greatest of all stations in England."

★ Sheffield and the train spotter

In Great Britain, railway fans are called trainspotters or anoraks, named after their typical choice of clothing. As a young man, Michael Palin, once a member of the Monthy Python troupe and now a producer of BBC world travel documentaries, was a trainspotter. From his home station in Sheffield, he explored Central England. He often stayed at Retford station, where the Flying Scotsmen locomotives passed.

Newcastle

The northern English city of Newcastle upon Tyne is located at or above the Tyne River. On the steep riverbank, there was a castle until the 19th century once used to defend the town against the Scots. Yet, since the space near the river is so narrow, the castle had to be demolished to enable the construction of the train station in the middle of the 19th century. Queen Victoria attended the opening in August 1850. South of the river lies Gateshead, and the two cities are connected by two railway bridges over the Tyne. The first bridge was designed by Robert Stephenson (1803-1859), the only son of the locomotive pioneer George Stephenson.

Warrington - No kissing!

On 13 February 2009, just in time for Valentine's Day, "No Kissing" signs were in Warrington´s Bank Quay Station as part of refurbishing measures. These are primarily meant for the parking spaces and the station taxi ranks. Since the introduction of faster Pendolino trains between London and Scotland, the number of passengers in the station had grown strongly, resulting in traffic congestion in front of the station due to couples kissing goodbye repeatedly. A French blogger said that the ban would not be surprising because of the English aversion to sex. The local authorities said they would certainly not be enforcing the ban rigidly. By the way, the model for this measure was the Chicago suburb of Deerfield station, where in 1979, a no-kissing zone was set up. Soon enough, the national news and U.S. media, such as TIME magazine, reported on the story.

No-Kissing-sing at Warrington station

★ Milton and the paper tickets

In 1836, Thomas Edmondson (1792-1851) became head of the small, newly built station nearby Milton (now Brompton station) on the railway line Newcastle-Carlisle. Edmondson, however, was bothered by the little pieces of paper that, taken from the stagecoach era, had been issued as tickets up until then. He began to assemble a machine, which produced small cardboard tickets, which were about 3 inches wide and 5.7 cm long. Additionally, Edmondson made a box for storing the tickets and a press for the dating of the tickets. This production system was not only beneficial for the tickets, but also for the control, accounting, and audit of the sales. Therefore, other stations soon followed his methods, and Edmondson was promoted to director of the Manchester and Leeds Railway. The system was eventually introduced at all stations of this network. Finally, it spread throughout Europe. At German secondary rail lines, it was used for almost 150 years long and survived till the 1980s under the name Edmondsche Pappfahrkarten. Even today, those tickets are used by museum railways for nostalgic reasons, such as the Harz Narrow Gauge Railway.

Sunderland Monkwearmouth

Once, the station of the northern English city of Sunderland was located in the Monkwearmouth district. With its pillars and its portal in the classical style, the station building was one of the finest in the country. It can still be admired today as a museum, with elements from the early 20th century Edwardian era. The reason for the magnificent expansion of Monkwearmouths in the 1840s was the ambition of the local railroad financier and parliamentarian George Hudson (1800-1871), who was also called "Railway King." Yet, in the 1850s, the first British railway bubble burst, and the truth also came out that Hudson had bribed other MPs. Thus, his fate soon turned against him, and he had to spend several years in exile on the Continent.

The station was beautifully preserved for a long time. However, in 1967, the Beeching Axe' savings measures of the British railways - named after Richard Beeching, the author of a report on potential savings in the railway network - put an end to train traffic, and the station was converted into a museum.

★ Appleby (-in-Westmoreland) and the Bishop

On 13 May 1978, the Anglican Bishop Eric Treacy suffered a heart attack at the station of Appleby (-in-Westmoreland) in North England (Cumbria) and died. He had participated in a nostalgic rail tour, where the last steam locomotive built by the British Railways, the BR 92 220 Evening Star, was used. A memorial plaque in the train station reminds passersby of him because Treacy was popular and well known by railway workers. He was not only a clergyman but also a respected railway photographer in England. When photographing, he wore a white bracelet so that the train staff saw him. They also provided him with interesting information about trains, which he photographed. He returned the favor with prints of his images for references. His 12,000 railway photographs were donated to the National Railway Museum in York.

★ Kingston upon Hull and Philip Larkin

Philip Larkin (1922-1985) was one of the greatest English poets of the 20th century. Since 1955, he worked as a university librarian in the English town of Hull North. On Saturday, the 13th of August, 1955, Larkin went by train from Hull Paragon station to London. This trip inspired the popular poem "The Whitsun Weddings."

That Whitsun, I was late getting away:
Not till about
One-twenty on the sunlit Saturday
Did my three-quarters-empty train pull out,
All windows down, all cushions hot, all sense
Of being in a hurry gone. We ran
Behind the backs of houses, crossed a street
Of blinding windscreens, smelt the fish-dock; thence
The river's level drifting breadth began,
Where sky and Lincolnshire and water meet.

In 2010, to mark the 25th anniversary of the poet's death, a statue of Larkin was installed at the Hull station (sculptor Martin Jennings). Jennings had also created the statue of Betjeman in London's St. Pancras station. In the shadow of the statue of Larkin, it reads,
"That Whitsun, I was late getting away..."

Alnwick Station and the bookstore

The city centre railway station of Alnwick in northern England was built in 1887 and closed in the late 1980s. The building has, however, been preserved in its original state, and in 1991, a large second-hand bookshop called Barter Books (2700 m2) was opened there. *The New Statesman* described Barter as "The British Library of secondhand bookshops."

Crewe - the trainspotter Mecca

Britain is considered the king of traffic observers. There are not only trainspotters, but even plane spotters, bus spotters, and canal spotters (gongoozlers). The most numerous of the groups are trainspotters - also called anoraks because of their typical choice of clothes - with around 200,000. Crewe, a station in the North West of England near Manchester, is considered a Mecca for British trainspotters. Built in 1837, the Crewe railway station, due to its well-preserved historic features, is considered one of the most interesting stations in the world as regards to the quality of its technical heritage. Crewe was the first station with its own hotel, which opened in 1838 and still exists today. Crewe also attracts railway fans as a railway junction with very complex track plans and ancient platform access. However, the historic facilities have one downside; in 2008, train passengers chose Crewe as one of Britain's ten worst railway stations to change trains.

Crewe Station (picture: Wikipedia)

4.4 Scotland

Edinburgh Waverley and the novel

Edinburgh's main railway station (Waverley Station) is located in a valley in the middle of the city. 38,000 passengers use the station every day, and covering one hectare of land, it is the second-largest station in the UK. It is also the only station in the country which is named after a novel. Sir Walter Scott (1771-1832) was a famous novelist, and, in some ways, was even the first writer with an international career. In 1814, he wrote his first novel anonymously called *Waverly*. In the novel, Waverly is the name of the protagonist. The book was a great success, and the following novels were also successful, but he still published them anonymously as the "author of *Waverly*." However, it soon became clear who was behind these novels. Later, the train station in Edinburgh was named after this book.

Station and Hotel

☞ Adjacent to Waverley Station is the luxurious Balmoral Hotel (5 star). This hotel was built in 1902 and has a highly visible clock tower. The minute hand of the clock is always, however, running two minutes ahead of time (except on New Year's Eve), so that passengers do not miss the train.

Edinburgh Haymarket and the French accent

Before the tunnel to the Waverly station had been built in 1846, Haymarket Station - the terminus of the Glasgow-Edinburgh line - was opened in 1842. In the last few years, Haymarket has seen an increase in travellers by 50 percent to 1.6 million passengers annually. Is the increase due to Vincent Houplain, a Frenchman who moved to Scotland in 2001 because of a Scottish woman and now reads the announcements in this station? The commuters are surprised by the French accent of the announcements, and there are already Houplain fans, especially women, who find his accent "sexy."

☞ The Haymarket train station is actually one of the few who has a track numbered with 0.

Glasgow - Heilanman's Umbrella

Opened in 1879, Glasgow Central Station has two levels of track. This was an advantage in 2002, as the lower level flooded after heavy rains. The glass-enclosed bridge over Argyle Street Station also offers weather protection. It has, therefore, been nicknamed *Heilanman's umbrella*, as it was once a popular meeting place of Highlanders that had moved to Glasgow.

Jordan Hill and Wikipedia

Jordan Hill is a suburban district of Glasgow and, according to Wikipedia, since 1887, has a railway station. The corresponding Wikipedia entry (by the computer scientist Ewan MacDonald) was the one millionth Wikipedia page written in English. This fact and the related fame, however, has also meant that the webpage has often been altered and erroneous information was added. Some locals want to equip the Jordan Hill station with a memorial plaque to remind passersby about its Wikipedia entry.

Dingwall and the tea

In the north of Scotland, near Inverness in the Highlands, the Kyle of Lochlash railway line joins the Far North Line. Here lies the small railway station Dingwall. In the First World War, many soldiers and sailors traveled through the station, where they were cheered up by the Red Cross with a cup of tea. At the station, a brass plaque with the following inscription has been applied: "This railway station was used as a tea stall for sailors and soldiers from 20th September 1915 until 12th April 1919, during which period, 134,864 men were supplied with tea."

4.5 Wales and the Island of Man

Llanfairpwll ...

To increase appeal to tourists, the North Wales village of Llanfairpwll acquired a very long name in the 19th century: Llanfairpwllgwyngyllgogerychwyrndrobwillantysilioogofg och. This was not without effect, as more tourists get out at the station to be photographed next to the odd long station sign.

Snaefell Mountain Railway and the visibility

On clear days, one can see Ireland, Scotland, England, and Wales from the mountain station (built in 1895) of the 8 km long 1067 mm narrow gauge Snaefell Mountain Railway on the Isle of Man.

4.6 Northern Ireland

Belfast Central Railway Station

Belfast has several train stations. Despite the name, the Central Railway Station is on the outskirts of town. This is because the station was not named after its location but after the Belfast Central Railway company. Much closer to central Belfast is, however, the Great Victoria Street Station.

Waterside Station

Once, there were three terminal stations in the city of Londonderry/Derry, but after two closed, only one remained. This station, originally called Londonderry Waterside station, now is simply named Londonderry station. The name of the town and its station is certainly a political issue. While the British and loyal Protestants call the city Londonderry, Catholics call it just Derry.

4.7 Republic of Ireland

From Kingsbridge to Heuston

In 1966, on the 50th Anniversary of the Irish Easter Rising, the Dublin train stations were renamed to remember rebels executed by the British in 1916. The former Kingsbridge Station in the west of Dublin (opened in 1848) was renamed Heuston station (after Sean Heuston [1891-1916], who was executed). Additionally, the central and busiest railway station was renamed Connolly Station after James Connolly (1868-1916).

From Dublin to Oslo

In Dublin's Connolly station, there is a bar called Oslo. In early 2007, the toilets in the train station closed due to repairs. At the toilet entrance, hung a sign saying, "Closed for repairs. Please use the toilets of Oslo. "

Tralee - Europe's most westerly station

From Dublin's Heuston station, some trains head towards Tralee, the westernmost station in Europe. Tralee is near the 10th Longitude west of Greenwich, and therefore, further west than any station in Portugal. When the station was opened in 1859, it was called South Tralee. Like the train stations in Dublin, it was also officially re-named Casement Station in 1966 after an Irish insurgent, who was executed by the British in 1916. However, unlike in Dublin, there is only one station in Tralee. Therefore, the term did not gain traction, and the local population simply says Tralee station.

The strange path of Listowel

From Tralee to Listowel, there are only buses. From 1888 to 1924, the first monorail line, the Listowel-Ballybunion Railway, was connected to Tralee station. Its inventor, the Frenchman Charles Lartigue, also built a 90 km stretch in the Algerian desert in the 19th Century. It was, hence, referred to as Lartigue Monorail.

The Irish monorail was only 10 miles long, and its construction cost 30,000 Pounds. For journeys, it had to be ensured that the left and right seated passengers had about the same weight. Despite these balance requirements, even cows were transported. In the Irish Civil War, the rail car was damaged, and soon after, the line was abandoned. However, a short section has been reconstructed in 2008.

★ Bundoran and the change of times

Located on the coast of Donegal in northwestern Ireland, the small town of Bundoran (1700 inhabitants) got a railway station in 1866. In 1957, the station was demolished, and a car park was built in its place. It is actually a shame that the station no longer exists given its significance to a monumental change - one that many railroad experts also are unaware of - that affects railroad timetables around the world to this day.

One day in 1872, the Scottish railroad engineer Sandford Fleming (1827-1915) stayed in Bundoran. At 17:25, he wanted to travel by train to Belfast. Yet, Fleming waited in vain for the train because the timetable contained an error. The train did not leave at 5:25 pm, but rather at 5:25 am. Fleming was forced to spend a night in the small town and began to reflect on how the effects of such small misprints could be reduced. Since Canadian railways, where Fleming was employed (Fleming was involved in the construction of the first transcontinental railroad in Canada), also had problems with local times and time zones, Fleming came up with the idea of a universal world standard time and the introduction of time zones. Moreover, the timetables should number the hours from 0-24, instead of 0-12. Instead of 5:25 pm, one would read 17:25 to avoid problems similar to those experienced by Fleming in Bundoran. In 1879, Fleming proposed his Universal Standard Time to the Royal Canadian Institute, and in 1884, the Universal Standard Time had been accepted worldwide. Even the current time zones in the U.S. and Canada originate with Fleming.

☞ Curiously, the inventive Fleming designed an early version of the skateboard in 1850.

5. Southern Europe

5.1 Italy (incl. San Marino and Vatican City)

The station at the Vatican

With an area of only 0.44 km^2, Vatican city is the smallest country in the world. However, it still has a railway station. The Lateran Treaty of 1929 between Italy and the Holy See stated that the new state should be provided with a rail connection. In 1934, the connection was opened. This required the walls of the Vatican to be broken, and since then, a large metal gate closes off the passage. A 100 m of the railway line within the walls of the Vatican belongs to the Holy See, while the 600-meter long link outside the Vatican belongs to the Italian State Railways FS. The Italian government pays for the infrastructure and provides the vehicles, while the Vatican pays the operation costs. The tracks lead to San Pietro Station, from which there is a connection to the former papal seat Viterbo. However, the railway line has only seen little traffic since its opening. Today, it is mainly used by freight trains—with an average of six cars—which provide employees with goods. The relatively small station Vatican City is clad inside with marble and travertine. In 2002, John Paul II boarded a train there that would take him to Assisi. However, a petrol station in the Vatican, where selected citizens can refuel exempt from petrol tax, makes significantly more sales than this station.

San Marino's former railway

While Hitler was focused on road construction, the Italian dictator Mussolini (1883-1945) acted as a railroad aficionado. Even today, there is the saying in Italy, that under

Mussolini, at least the trains ran on time. Under "Il Duce," the Vatican and San Marino were connected to the railway network. In December 1928, construction began for a sinuous electric narrow-gauge railway from Rimini to San Marino City. The 32 km long railway line was opened in 1932. The line was destroyed in 1944 by Allied bombing. Between 1958 and 1960, the line was dismantled. Some of the route had to give way to a fast road, while a short distance was converted to a bike path. In the lower town of San Marino (a cable car connects it with the upper town), there are still remnants of the former station building.

Milano Centrale - the emulated imitation

At the beginning of the 20th century, new monumental terminal stations in Europe and North America were trying to surpass each other. Many decided to copy historical models or other contemporary structures. The Central Station of Milan, whose completion was delayed for political and economic reasons, was meant to be the last large bang of the era of great new stations. It tried to outdo all existing stations when it opened in 1935. It was modeled after the Union Station in Washington, which, in turn, was modeled after the Arch of Constantine. The resulting architectural style and its oversized dimensions were a mixed-up creation, in fact, a copy of an American copy of Roman architecture. It was quite difficult to classify, and locals called it Assyro-Milanese. The architectural style is sometimes attributed to Mussolini, but at his time, Italy was already building more modern, as the Santa Maria Novella train station in Florence (completed in 1934) shows.

Roma Termini and the Osram lamp

With half a million users per day, Roma Termini is the

busiest train station in southern Europe. As early as the 1930s, construction of the new terminus station on Esquiline Hill began, and the side buildings were built according to plans by the architect Mazzoni. The main passenger building, however, was only realized in the early 1950s. It was built in a modern style and designed by a team of six architects. This off-setting building was later given the nickname "dinosauro (dinosaurs)." For all the modernity, however, the building offered no prominent meeting place. This was finally found by users in the form of a high lamp in the plaza in front of the station, nicknamed the Lampada Osram. The Lampada Osram was initially a meeting point of Sardinians and later, of Asian immigrants. There are even Italian songs mentioning the lamp.

The flat station of Naples

In 1954, a competition for the redesign of the facilities of the central station of Naples at the Piazza Garibaldi was held. Important Italian architects took part. The famous engineer Pier Luigi Nervi proposed a large station hall. However, none of these proposals were implemented. The reason for this was the intention of not obstructing the view of Vesuvius. Finally, the design office of the State railway came up with a simple plan, which just featured a flat roof.

In Afragola, a suburb of Naples, a new high-speed train station designed by the British-Iraqi architect Zaha Hadid has opened. It was scheduled to open in 2011, but because of delays, the opening took place only in 2017. Again, this spectacular station crouches with its flat roof in the countryside of Campania.

Turin - the train station late celebration

The Turin's Porta Nuova train station, with over 190,000 passengers per day, is the third busiest train station in Italy behind Roma Termini and Milano Centrale. The modern station was only officially inaugurated in February 2009. However, already in December 1864, the first trains departed from the station. However, at that time, the people of Turin were not in a mood to celebrate. The city's mood was hampered after learning that it would lose its capital status to the more centrally located Florence. Because the unification of Italy started in the northwest of the country, Turin was originally unified Italy's first capital. However, it was obvious that the city could not cling to this role forever.

★ The monument at the Brenner

The greatest work of the Swabian railway engineer Karl Etzel was the construction of the Brenner railway line between 1864 and 1867. However, Etzel died before the completion of the project. In November 1864, he had his first stroke. Therefore, he asked for his release from the project and was planning to settle down in the villa he designed for himself in Bad Cannstatt. Yet, while sitting on the train from Vienna to Stuttgart in May 1865, he had to interrupt his voyage because of a second stroke. He got out at Kemmelbach station, where he died shortly afterwards. Etzel's tomb in the Prag-cemetery in Stuttgart was built from various rocks from Brenner. In 1892, on the 25th Anniversary of the Brenner railway, a memorial for Etzel was inaugurated in the Brenner railway station. The station offered little space, but under an arch of the platform roof, they found room for the bust. After the First World War, the Brenner station became Italian. Therefore, the Italians added an Italian-language version of the inscription on the Etzel monument.

★ Bruno Bruni and Gradara

Gradara is a very simple train stop on the mainline from Rimini to Ancona. If one gets off here, one sees a caretaker cottage standing close to the tracks. The painter and graphic artist Bruno Bruni (born in 1935) grew up here. Today, Bruni is today one of the most famous Italian artists living in Germany. After returning home from World War I disabled, Bruni's father got a job as a railway attendant. When trains were passing close to the house, the cups on the kitchen table shook. Bruno got so used to the proximity of the railway as a child that he would later in life not fall asleep without train noise. Later, the railway again impacted his destiny: he met his current girlfriend at the main station of Hanover.

Bologna and the clock that stopped running

Bologna is a central node in the Italian railway network: an important hub for north-south and east-west lines. Neo-fascist terrorists chose the station in 1980 for an atrocity to shake the country. On 2 August 1980, a suitcase with a 20 kg TNT bomb placed at a wall in the waiting room exploded. Eighty-five people, including many tourists in transit, died, and 200 people were injured. The right wing of the station building was completely destroyed. The middle section of the building remained largely intact. The clock in the central portion of the station stood still at the time of the explosion (10:25). It was never set in motion again, and hence, still reminds those in the station of the time when the atrocity happened.

Foggia and the stalagmite

In Puglia, a karst region, there are many caves. The largest, the Grotte di Castellana, was astonishingly first discovered in 1938. Earlier, a hole in the earth was known, which was used by the local population as a garbage dump. When the speleologist Franco Anelli discovered the cave on 23 January 1938, it took another twelve years to remove the garbage thrown into the hole. Today, the cave is an important tourist attraction of Puglia. One can walk about three kilometers deep into it. In the station hall of Foggia, a stalagmite gives testimony to the wealth of the caves of Puglia. However, Foggia lies about 100 km from Castellana Grotto. Putting such a stalagmite to a station closer to the caves, such as Bari, would have been more appropriate.

Trieste Centrale and its German architect

The architecture of the main station of Trieste (Trieste Centrale) looks Italian, yet was built by German speakers. Its architect, William von Flattich, came from Stuttgart, and the station was built for the Austrian Southern Railway in 1878. Trieste, which was still a part of Austria at that time, was an important port of the Habsburg Empire.

Trieste Campo Marzio

Trieste once even had a more splendid station called Campo Marzio. It was the terminus of the state-owned Bohinj railway line, also known as karst railway, which ran from Jesenice, through the Slovenian countryside to Trieste. Due to new state borders (Yugoslavia) after World War I, the station lost its importance and was shut down in 1959. Today, the dilapidated building houses a railroad museum.

5.2 Spain

Madrid Atocha and the tunnel

The Atocha station in Madrid's south is, with 450,000 passengers per day (including the subway passengers), the largest station in the Iberian Peninsula. An underground rail line connects it to the North Station Chamartin. The construction of this railway tunnel went on for so long that it got the nickname Tunel de la Risa (laughable tunnel) by the Madrilene. For World Expo 92, a fast rail link was opened to Seville, and plants from the botanical garden of the Expo were later taken to the station, making Atocha one of the few railway station concourses with palm trees. On 11 March 2004, the railway station made headlines around the world because of a terrorist attack. Today, a monument to the victims outside the railway station stands as a reminder of that date.

Valencia North Station

Valencia's central train station - designed by the Spanish architect Demetrio Ribes in a mixture of the Vienna Secession, Art Nouveau, and Moorish elements and opened in 1917 - is home to many strange anomalies. First, it is called North Station (Estacion dc Nortc), although it lies south of downtown. On the other hand, the connecting subway station is not called North Station, but rather Xativa. On the façade of the station, no less than 400 oranges can be seen. This harkens to Valencia's orange cultivation. It is also strange that the words "Good Travel" are displayed in eight languages along the walls of the main hall, but not in the former international language: French.

Valencia North Station

Canfranc - The Ghost Station

At the beginning of the 20th Century, there was a project for a fast connection between Paris and Madrid, which crossed the Pyrenees on the shortest route. Since France used standard gauge and Spain broad gauge, a transfer station was needed. A plateau north of the small Spanish village of Jaca, which lies south of the Pyrenees ridge, was identified as the best place for that project. As several thousand passengers per day were expected and facilities for transit and customs formalities had to be considered, a railway station compound with a generous layout and long roofed platforms was built and completed in 1925. Passengers were expected to get off at the end of a train station and, after passing through the border formalities, get back in on the other side. However, as a result of the world economic crisis and political tensions before the Second World War traffic, the station received far less traffic than expected. During the Second World War, there were rumors that the Nazis secretly brought hoards of gold here. After the war, the rail line still operated but was no longer served by international fast traffic. In 1970, a bridge collapsed on the French side, marking the end of border-crossing operations. The old railway tunnel was then used for the construction of Somport road mountain pass, and the railway tunnel now houses an underground laboratory. The station also operated as the terminus station for a few regional trains from Zaragoza. Currently, the station building is vacant and is repeatedly explored by iron rail enthusiasts. However, renovation works in the station have started.

Linares and the upturned wagon

Old Train Station in Linares (image: Escuela de Estudios Flamenco)

The Spanish city of Linares used to be on the Cordoba-Marid long-distance line. However, since the opening of the high-speed line Madrid-Seville, most long-distance trains bypass the city. Six slower long-distance trains still connect the station Linares-Baeza, however, no trains depart anymore. The former station is now home to a conservatory, which is dedicated to the study of flamenco. The former station building has two corner turrets with round windows, which look like railway wheels. The upper floor of the station thus looked like a railroad car, lying on his back. Some suggest that this was intended by the architect Narciso Claria.

Seville and the cold shower

In the final film by Mexican director Luis Buñuel (1900-1983), "That Obscure Object of Desire," the protagonist Mathieu, a mature Frenchmen, pours a bucket of water over the head over his young coveted Spanish lover Conchinta before the train leaves the Seville station to Paris. Then he has to explain his actions to the other passengers in the compartment.

Miranda de Ebro and the priest

Miranda de Ebro is a major railway transport hub in northern Spain. Here, the railway lines Irun-Madrid-Barcelona and Bilbao cross. To prevent the above-ground crossing of the tracks, subways to the platforms were created in this station. However, passengers had to get used to them. One day, in 1971, the following announcement was transmitted by the station: "Dear passengers, the train from Bilbao to Zaragoza will shortly arrive on track 2. Do not cross the tracks. Please use the subways." Yet, a priest in a cassock walked straight across the track. He probably had not heard the announcement. The staff in the control room of the station must have seen him because, suddenly, a new announcement echoed through the station saying, "And this bastard priest was just the first one who ran on the tracks." The railway officials had forgotten to turn off the microphone.

Bilbao - the city's sights traffic

The Basque industrial city of Bilbao is famous for its spectacular Guggenheim Museum. Additionally, the city of

Bilbao also has many traffic-related sights. In Bilbao, there is not only a tram and a subway, but the city also has a transporter bridge and funicular railways. Additionally, Bilbao has two stations, which are among the most interesting in Europe. These are the Abando station, with its large glass mosaic built in 1902, and the Concordia station, with its finely crafted facade of the Belle Epoque period.

Concordia Station in Bilbao (Image: Wikipedia)

The station with the silver track

The first railway line of the Spanish kingdom was opened in 1837 in Cuba. In 1848, the first line of the Iberian Peninsula followed between Barcelona and Mataro. The first railway tracks in the Madrid region were laid in 1851 to Aranjuez, where there was a royal palace. However, the queen demanded that the palace should be reached by tracks made from silver. Hence, rail made of silver was laid for the final meters. Yet, the very next day, the silver tracks were replaced by those of iron.

This railway line was soon popular with the Madrilene. In the neighborhood of Aranjuez, there were fields with delicious strawberries. Thus, the train to Aranjuez was soon called "Tren de las Fresas (strawberry train)."

★ Segovia-Guiomar

When a new high-speed train station was built in Segovia, far from the city centre, a name for the new station had to be found. The following criteria were given for the name: it should be a female, it should have something to do with the history of the city, and it should have no religious connotations. Finally, they agreed on Guiomar. Guiomar is a character in the work of Spanish writer Antonio Machado (1875-1939). Machado often came by train to Segovia, spent several years there, and had a secret lover: Pilar Valderrama, the married mother of three children. In his books, he called her Guiomar.

Lisbon's diverse traffic

Lisbon is an interesting city when it comes to transportation because of the great variety of transportation modes available. In addition to modern and ancient trams, there are funicular railways, a cable car, a free-standing public elevator, subways, and ferries. In rail transport, there are also suburban trains, three terminal stations, and other railway stations, including the modern Oriente Station built for the Expo 98 by the Spanish architect Santiago Calatrava. The massive concrete structures inside the station give the feeling of moving in the skeleton of a dinosaur.

Inside the Oriente Station of Lisbon

Lisbon's unfortunate station

The Cais do Sodre train station in Lisbon can be seen as persecuted by bad luck. In the 1950s, a lighthouse fell from the train station at the end of the suburban railway line to Cascais (the westernmost station on the European mainland) and killed eight passengers. In 1961, a bomb was detonated by a terrorist in the station. In May 1963, a loud noise again shook the city. The station roof collapsed, killing 49 people. Cranes and other equipment had to be removed from the building site of the large Abril bridge to lift the wreckage away. During subway construction in the late 1990s, there were landslides at the station, which delayed its completion.

☞ But even in the Rossio station, built in 1890 in the Neo Manueline style, not everything works. This station was stylishly restored in 2006 but was not opened until the spring of 2008, as the refurbishment of the tunnel to the station was delayed. The construction company wanted to delay its completion to 2011 but was urged to speed up.

Due to problems with the tunnel construction of the subway station, the Santa Apollonia terminal station was also delayed.

Porto São Bento

In 1903, the Porto São Bento railway station, with its French Renaissance design, was opened. The terminal station is known for its 20,000 blue tiles (azulejos) in the station hall, which depict scenes of Portuguese history. Because the topography of Porto is complicated, the railway line leading out of the station disappears in a tunnel and a little later, crosses the Douro river on a concrete bridge that replaced an iron bridge built by Gustav Eiffel in the 1990s. In the 19th century, there were several suggestions for routes to downtown. When one of the tunnels was already completed, it was decided to change the route. Thus, the building was converted into a wine cellar for the local port.

Porto São Bento

Portugal and the insect station

Portugal has a relatively small rail network, with a length of only about 2600 km. In the last two decades, with the help of EU funding, large portions of the network were modernized, and stations were restored. The smooth, shiny granite floors of many stations look neat but are fatal to many insects. Since the insects fly at night towards the neon tubes on the ceiling, they fall to the ground and remain on their back. When they attempt to regain their footing, the slippery floor offers no friction allowing them to flip over.

5.5 Greece

Thessaloniki

While the main station of the Greek capital Athens, Larissa Station, is relatively small, Thessaloniki has the largest station building of the country. It was built under Prime Minister Ioannis Metaxas, who led the government from 1936 to 1941 in an increasingly dictatorial way. Impressed by the new railway station buildings in Mussolini's Italy, Metaxas also wanted something monumental to show off in Greece. In front of the massive train station, however, one finds a relatively modest steam engine, which is reminiscent of the beginnings of the railway industry in Greece. In the station itself, there is even an Orthodox chapel.

★ Volos - the former narrow-gauge rail junction

The central Greek city of Volos (now 82,000 inhabitants) was only a small town for a long time. However, when Greece got Thessaly back from the Ottoman Empire in 1881, the city rapidly developed. It soon got a station, and its mix of styles, with non-Greek Balkan and Middle Eastern elements, still surprises today. The Italian Evaristo de Chirico was the architect. His son, Giorgio de Chirico (1888-1978), born in Volos, later became a famous Italian surrealist painter. Another special feature of the Volos train station used to be the meeting of three gauges: a standard gauge line, a meter-gauge line, and the 600 mm narrow-gauge line of Volos-Milies, the Mt. Pelion Railway. A section Mt. Pelion Railway, from Lechonie to Miles, is still present and on weekends used by tourist trains.

☞Another station built by Chirico can be found in Ana Lechonia, 11 km east of Volos.

5.5 Cyprus and Malta

Famagusta steam locomotive

In Cyprus, there are no passenger rail services today. In front of the accounting office in Famagusta in the Turkish part of the island, however, stands a steam locomotive, indicating that there was once on the island railway. The accounting office is, in fact, a former railway station. Starting in Famagusta, there was a 60 kilometers long narrow-gauge railway (762 mm) to Nicosia and Morphou. This route was used mainly for freight, as Cyprus was rich in mineral resources (the name of the island, Kypros, is derived from the Greek word for copper). On 31 December 1951, the last passenger train left Nicosia. The route of the railway is now in the UN buffer zone, and there is nothing more to see of the track. The railway also ran through the Famagusta bathing suburb of Varoscha, which took on the character of a ghost town after 1974 when it was divided.

Malta's short-lived railway

Even Malta once had a railroad. The Maltese railway connected Valetta with Mdina in the island's interior. It was opened in 1883 but closed down in 1931. In 1903, in a tram from Valetta's main station to the hinterland opened, which was also shut down in 1929. The rail traffic on both networks disappeared, and the railway station in Valetta was bombed during World War II. But the route into the old town - leading over a bridge, into a tunnel, and an incision in the city wall - in which the city's train station was located, can still be seen today. The densely populated and highly motorized Malta is now drowning in road traffic, and the reintroduction of a tram is, therefore, being discussed.

6. Central and Eastern Europe

<u>6.1 Poland</u>

Warsaw Central Railway Station

Warsaw was almost entirely destroyed by the Germans in World War II. The old town and castle were later rebuilt true to the originals, but city planners opted for a new building for the central station (the previous building was opened in 1939). The construction was begun in 1972 and needed to be ready before a visit from Leonid Breschnew in 1975. Therefore, it was built very hastily. Shortly after the opening, the building started showing some initial damages. The bulky, inelegant building is now considered a white elephant in the western city center. At the time of its opening, the station was still shining with innovations that were still quite rare in the Eastern bloc, such as escalators and automatic doors. On the other hand, there are still not even ticket machines at the station. Since 1989, the station has gone rather downhill. The competition from road, air, and bus travel has reduced traffic by rail significantly.

★ Wroclaw railway station

Wroclaw has a beautiful train station, which survived the war almost unscathed but suffered some from floods. In the station, a plaque embedded into the floor and unveiled by the Polish director Andrzej Wajda (1997) recalls a tragic accident that took place here in 1967.

The actor Zbigniew Cybulski (1927-1967) was very popular in Poland and was seen as a Polish James Dean. While James Dean died in 1955 in a car accident, Cybulski died in a train accident in 1967. While James Dean died in a fancy Porsche car, it was a train that cost Cybulski his life. Cybulski tried heroically to jump on a train leaving for Warsaw. However, he slid off and fell under its wheels.

Gdansk railway station

The tower at the Gdansk railway station slightly mimics the architecture of the municipal city hall's right tower. This tower was originally built in a Gothic style, but after a fire in the 16th Century, it was rebuilt in the style of Mannerism (Renaissance-Baroque transition).

☞ In front of the Gdańsk station, the sculptor Frank Meisler (1925-2018) created a memorial to remember World War II's children's transport. In August 1939, Meisler himself even succeeded with other Jewish children to flee from Danzig in a railway cattle car, eventually arriving in London via Berlin.

Lodz and the station name

The Lodz head railway station, built by Adolf Schimmelpfennig in 1868, was called "Lodz Fabryczna (Lodz Factory)" because there were many textile factories not far from the station. In the 19th century, the development of the textile city attracted several entrepreneurs, including the Rhinelander Karl Scheibler, who had become an industrial baron in Lodz and who promoted the city's rail connection and the construction of train stations. His hometown Montjoie was renamed Monschau in 1918 because the original name sounded too French. His new home Lodz was also to be renamed under the Nazis, and the train station itself became Litzmannstadt center. By the way, Lodz is called "Boat," and one of these is also found on the city arms. Today, the Lodz Fabryczna railway station has been renovated and the city will soon get an underground rail starting from here.

Kutno station

Kutno is one of the most important stations in the district of Lodz. However, it does not have a good reputation. The Polish cult rock band sang about it:
Were you ever at night in the station of Kutno?
There it is so dirty and ugly, that you can't believe your eyes.

★ Posen

On 25 November 2006, the Polish journalist and travel writer Ryszard Kapuscinski (1932-2007) revealed a commemorative plaque in the entrance hall of the station Poznan for the globetrotter Kazimierz Nowak who died (1897-1937) in Poznan from malaria. From 1931 to 1936, Nowak crossed Africa from north to south, covering a distance of 40 000 km, alone on foot and by bicycle. The plaque at the station shows his route.

Korschen and soup

Korsze (formerly known as Korschen) was an East Prussian railway junction prior to World War II. Here, the steam locomotive water tanks were filled up. Steam trains to Berlin had a twenty minute water refilling stop, giving everyone just enough time for a snack. The station restaurant adapted to this situation and offered a tasty soup. This was soon so well known throughout Germany that a hotel in Berlin had a potato soup called "à la Korschen" on the menu.

6.2 Czech Republic

Prague - The many names of the station

Prague's main train station has had many names. When it was opened in 1871, Bohemia was still a part of Austria, and the station was called Kaiser Franz Joseph Station. After the First World War, the Czech Republic and Slovakia, which previously belonged to Hungary, became independent as Czechoslovakia, and the station was named Wilson-Bahnhof out of gratitude to the American President Woodrow Wilson (1856-1924). Under the German occupation and after the Second World War, the station was simply called "train station (hlavni nadrazi in Czech)." After 1989, efforts were made to rename the station back to Wilson station, but due to railway authorities, the name has not changed.

Architects, in turn, call the station Fanta station. The name is due to the architect Josef Fanta (1856-1954), who designed the station's 1901-1909 Art Nouveau style. Today, the Art Nouveau part is separated from the city by a street, and you have to enter it through uncomfortable underground levels.

Sherwood Forest in Prague

In front of the Prague main railway station, there is a small park, which was the focal point of the homeless and drug addicts for a long time. Because of the feeling of insecurity, the Prague people gave it the nickname "Sherwood Forest" because, like Robin Hood, some people take (passers-by) and others give here.

★ Anton Dvorak and the Franz Joseph Station

The Czech composer Antonin Dvorak (1841-1904) was regarded as a railfan. He often went to Prague's main railway station and counted passing locomotives. He even asked his students for locomotive numbers. A job in the USA when he learned that he could watch the locomotives of the New York train station. In 1892, he took up the post of Director of the National Conservatory of Music in New York. However, New York disappointed him because watching trains passing was not possible in the former Grand Central Terminal. In 1895, Dvorak went back to Prague. In early 1904, he went to the Prague Franz-Joseph Station to observe trains. He came back to his apartment with a cold. A short time later, the composer and locomotive fan died.

☞ In 1919, by the way, the Franz Joseph statue was removed from the station, which had been renamed Wilson Station by that time.

Prague Tesnov station

Prague was spared from the destruction of the Second World War but mourned the loss of a station that was once considered one of the most beautiful in Europe. The main building of the railway station Tesnov was blown up in 1985 to make way for a road overpass. However, the first blow symbolically failed.

The station was built in 1875 by Austrian architect Schlimp in the neo-renaissance style, with a triumph arch-like portal and was originally called North West Railway Station. After the First World War, it was even called Denis station after a French historian and connoisseur of Bohemia. During the Second World War, it was due to its location renamed Moldova station.

Prague Masaryk and the pneumatic tube

Masaryk Railway Station, close to downtown Prague, is the city's oldest railway station. Its name has also changed quite often. It has already been called the Prague terminal court, State-station, and Hibernerbahnhof. As in the interwar period, it has since 1990 been named after the first Czech President: Tomáš Masaryk. Because Prague has two other major railway stations, and terminal stations have disadvantages as regards to the organisation of train traffic, there were already plans for the closure of the station. In Prague, there was once a well-functioning, 55 km long subterranean pneumatic tube system. However, after a flood in 2002, the system was decommissioned. The pneumatic tube system connected the main post office with other post offices. In case the staff of the central tubular postal node felt hungry, they called the pneumatic tube station in the station Masaryk. In that station, there was a good snack bar with delicious sausages. The sausages had the proper shape for the tubes and arrived warm. Potato pancakes followed with the next capsule.

★ Kostomlaty and ‚Closely Watched Trains'

In 1966, the Czech film comedy *Closely Watched Trains* was produced. The film is based on the book with the same name by the Czech writer Bohumil Hrabal (1914-1997). It is about an adolescent who works at a train station during the Second World War. The story reflects the benefits of knowledge of rail operations, which Hrabal himself had acquired in World War II. At that time, he was serving as an operating head of the station Kostomlaty nad Labem.

☞ Hrabal died in 1997 when he fell from the fifth-floor window of a hospital when feeding pigeons.

6.3 Slovakia

Bratislava and the greenhouse

Bratislava is limited in its expansion by mountain ranges, and for a long time, it had a relatively small railway station. Finally, in 1988, a new, larger building was erected. However, little effort was made for its design. The glass facade is broken by a massive roof and a similar style balcony. Because of the glass facade, the building was popularly nicknamed "greenhouse (sklenik)." However, there are plans to demolish the "greenhouse" and replace it with a modern building with integrated shopping facilities and underground tram lines.

Zariecie Žilina - the Art Station

The northern Slovak city of Zilina is currently going through an economic boom as a result of a major investment by the Korean automaker Kia. The Zariecie station went through ups and downs in its recent history. During the Third Reich, 18,000 Slovak Jews were sent from here to Auschwitz, which is about 150 km away. From 1946 to 1982, a family of railroaders with five children lived in the station. The family had animals, and the users of the station were served with cherries from their garden. Later, when the station was renewed, the family was asked to move out of the premises. After the turn of the century, the station began to deteriorate, and graffiti spread. However, a Slovak cultural initiative in 2003 transformed the station into a cultural center with theater festivals, art workshops for children, etc. Meanwhile, the operation of trains continues. Trains stop here, and the waiting room for the trains is also still there.

6.4 Hungary

Budapest - Nyugati (Western railway station)

The Nyugati (Western) Railway Station is one of the three major railway stations of Budapest and was once a pioneer station. The first Hungarian train left from here in 1846, following 35 km along the Danube to Vac. The station building was built from 1874 to 1877 by the French company Eiffel, under Gustave Eiffel's supervision. When the station required renovation in the 1980s, McDonald's Corporation was found as an investor. In 1990, the fast-food company opened its first branch in a station. This restaurant is regarded as the fanciest McDonald's in the world. The cake comes from the traditional Budapest pastry shop Gerber. When an attached shopping mall opened in 2000, Nyugati also became the first station in Hungary with a shopping centre.

Budapest Keleti Pu (Eastern)

The designation of railway stations in Budapest according to cardinal points is not very consistent. The west station Nyugati pu is actually a northern station, and the south station Deli pu is actually a station in the west of the city. Only the eastern station Keleti pu is really in the eastern part of the city. Supposedly, the Keleti station used the old castle-like Lehrter Bahnhof in Berlin as a model. However, only the slightly oversized portal adorned with statues by James Watt and George Stephenson indicates the style of the former Lehrter station. Today, most people reach the station by an underground passage. When it opened in 1884, Keleti was considered one of the most modern stations in Europe, as it was one of the first in Europe with electric lighting and a central switchboard.

In 2001, the Sarah Connor music video "From Sarah with Love" was filmed at the station.

Hódmezövásárhelykutasipuszta and Piroschka

The 1955 film *I often think of Piroschka*—which was very successful in Germany—was produced with Liselotte Pulver and Gunnar Möller in the lead roles. The film is about a German exchange student who falls in love with the daughter of the station master, Piroschka, in the small Puszta town Hódmezövásárhelykutasipuszta. Even today, there are German nostalgia tourists who search in southern Hungary for the Piroschka station. Also, one will search in vain for landscapes and buildings that can be seen in the film. During the Cold War, the film could not be shot in Hungary. Instead, it was shot in the Vojvodina region, which once belonged to Hungary, but was then a part of Yugoslavia (even the German Winnetou films were produced in Yugoslavia).

Miskolc-Tisza and the Celts

The northern Hungarian industrial city of Miskolc has two major railway stations: the Gomori station and the beautiful Tiszai station. Both stations were designed by the outstanding Hungarian architect Ferenc Pfaff (1851-1913). Some believe that the Tiszai station would be located on the Tisza river, but this river does not flow through Miskolc. In fact, the station was named after the company that built it. The station was opened in 1901. When the foundations were excavated, archaeological discoveries showed that the area was once inhabited by Celtic tribes. ☞ While Miskolc-Tisza is one of the most beautiful train stations in Hungary outside of Budapest, Debrecen station built in 1961 in the style of socialist modernism is one of the ugliest in the country.

★ Balatonszarszo and the dead poet

On 3 December 1937, the Hungarian poet Attila Jozsef (1905-1937) was run over by a train in the Lake Balaton resort Szárszó. Friends of the poet spoke of an accident, but apparently, he had leaped in front of a freight train. As a child, Jozsef already had tried to commit suicide. Today, Jozsef is considered among the most important Hungarian poets of the 20th Century. In 1998, near the train station of Szárszó, a monument to the poet was erected. This shows a railway wheelset on one track, loaded with metal rods, bearing the letters of Jozsef's poems.

Sopron and the Raaberbahn

In Hungary, Sopron is known as "urbs fidelissima," which means faithful town. The name derives from the population deciding in a referendum to remain with Hungary after the First World War. However, the German-speaking region around the town, previously belonging to Hungary, became a part of Burgenland, therefore, Austria. The small town of Eisenstadt became Burgenland's capital. Sopron was headquarters of the Raab-Oedenburg-Eisenstadt Railway (ROeEE, Hungarian GySEV, Gyor is the Hungarian name for Raab) today called Raaberbahn, which even survived the Cold War. Traffic at the Sopron station is characterized by the yellow-green painted trains of the Raaberbahn, as well as trains of the ÖBB (Austrian Railways), but hardly any material from the Hungarian state railway MAV.

7. South Eastern Europe

7.1 Slovenia

★ James Joyce and the night in Ljubljana

In the summer of 1904, the young Irish writer James Joyce (1882-1941) and his girlfriend Nora travelled by train from Zurich to Trieste, where he was given a job as an English teacher. In Ljubljana, which at that time belonged to Austria, the couple got out of the train, thinking they were already in Trieste. Yet, by the time they had noticed their mistake, the train had already left the station. Therefore, they spent the night on a park bench near the station and continued their trip the next morning. Joyce had his first date with Nora (who, by the way, he would not marry until 1931) on 16 June 1904. His most famous novel *Ulysses* is all about that date. Today, James Joyce fans each year celebrate Bloomsday (named after the protagonist of *Ulysses*) on 16 June. On 16 June 2003 (2004 would have been the centennial), the Slovenes unveiled a floor plate at platform 1 reminding about James Joyce's involuntary stay in the station, nearly 100 years ago.

Joze Plecnik and Kamnik

Joze Plecnik (1872-1957) is considered the foremost Slovenian architect of the 20th Century. He particularly left his mark in Ljubljana, although he did not design railway stations there. However, he designed a hunting lodge called Kamniska Bistrica in 1932 for the Yugoslav King Alexander, located in the railroad town of Kamnik. Therefore, the construction of a railway yard became necessary. Plečnik recommended his student Vinko Glanz for this work. Since Plečnik was not completely satisfied with Glanz's draft, he changed the sketches himself. This way, Slovenia indirectly obtained a Plečnik-designed station.

7.2 Croatia

Zagreb

Zagreb´s railway station square is considered one of the most beautiful in Europe. In the 1980s, a shopping centre was built close to the station but was placed underground inn order not to interfere with the quality of urban space above ground. Zagreb's main railway station is also likely to be one of the few in Europe, where a niche for an altar for the Virgin Mary was inserted into the façade on the rail side. In the former Yugoslavia, ethnicity and religion were closely linked, and this altar shows the Croatians close relation to Catholicism.

☞ Opposite the station, there is the famous Hotel Regent Esplanade, which after its opening in 1925 became an important hotel on the Orient-Express route. Famous people such as Josephine Baker and Charles Lindbergh once stayed here.

Zagreb West Station

While the Zagreb main station gives a perfect historical picture from the city side, today, large electronic departure boards on the platform side show the technical progress. That is why station film scenes that take place in a different era are more likely to be shot in the West Railway Station of Zagreb today. In that station, the historic atmosphere remains undisturbed by modern information display installations.

★ Kumrovec and Tito

Josip Broz Tito (1892-1980) was born in the Croatian village of Kumrovec, which lies on a railway line on the border with Slovenia. From the train station of the village, Tito once left for the world. As a head of state, he often came back, sometimes to visit his home village accompanied by state guests. He then arrived in the village station with his luxurious Blue train. This train set today can still be seen (and rented) in Belgrade´s central station compound.

7.3 Serbia and Montenegro

Belgrade's Central Station

The main station of Belgrade was built in 1884 in the neo-classical style on the site of a former lagoon on the river Sava. Outside the station is a blue steam locomotive, which once drew the "Blue train," with which Tito travelled through Yugoslavia.

Belgrade Prokop and the concrete slab

Today, Belgrade's main train station is a bit away from the city center and, as a terminus, is not operationally ideal. Therefore, for several years, plans for a new transit station had been prepared. A part of the necessary underground lines has been realized, and there is also the new railway station Prokop. However, this station is also not ideal. It only consists of a huge concrete slab under which the trains stop, the access facilities are covered by graffiti, and a cold wind blows through the east-west-oriented station during winter. Prokop can, therefore, be regarded as the most unpleasant station in Europe. A real station building was not realized until recently. Lack of funds and the collapse of Yugoslavia contributed to that.

The underground station Vukov Spomenic

As the first station of the new railway junction of Belgrade and part of a commuter rail system, the central underground station Vukov Spomenic was opened by the then-President of Yugoslavia Slobodan Milosevic in 1995.

At 40 meters below street level and 65 m long escalators, the train station is one of the deepest below the surface in Europe. Given the smooth and modern look of the station, it is quite strange to see a turgid copper sculpture with motifs of Belgrade at the end of the underground platform, which hides a fire exit.

The film at the train station Sarganska Osmica

One of the most popular railways in Serbia is the Sarganska Osmica, which is also called "Šargane eight." This 760 mm narrow-gauge railway, whose route has the shape of a figure eight in one section, was once the continuation of the Bosnian Eastern Railway on the Serbian side (Bosnia had an extensive narrow-gauge network). In 1974, the line was shut down in Serbia but rebuilt as a tourist attraction in 1999. On the route, there is a new train station, that is meant to look older, called Golubici station. This was the backdrop for the film *Life is a Miracle* by the Bosnian-Serb director Emir Kusturica. Also near the train station, located at the Šargane Eight, is Mokra Gora, a village designed and developed by Kusturica, where he now lives himself.

The train station in Herceg Novi

The Montenegrin port city of Herceg Novi did not have a railway station until 1936. However, only 31 years later, the railway and the station had already closed. Emir Kusturica, in 1998, bought the station and tried to develop a cultural center. He was not so very successful. Since 2005, the building was converted into a hotel.

7.4 North Macedonia and Kosovo

Skopje - the stationary station clock

The 26th of July, 1963, is considered the worst day in the history of Skopje, North Macedonia. Early in the morning, a strong earthquake hit the city, and more than 1,000 people died. Around 80 percent of the buildings, including the railway station, were destroyed. The large station clock remained standing and stuck forever at 5:17, the time of the earthquake. Today, this station is a memorial to the disaster and annexed to a museum. The damage exceeded the economic capabilities of Yugoslavia, and an international wave of help poured in. At the same time, after the destruction of the Ottoman old town, there were ambitions to free the city from its "Balkan backwardness" and to turn it into a showcase for socialism. The famous Japanese architect Kenzo Tange (1913-2005) drew up a plan for rebuilding the city. While the plans were realized only in part, Tange was able to prevail with the idea of an elevated station platform. Today, the trains run above the city, and a bus station is located at street level. After the fall of Yugoslavia, rail traffic fell sharply. Additionally, the concrete slab of the building is already showing signs of age. The bus station now takes on the brunt of the traffic.

Pristina Fushe Kosovë

Pristina, Kosovo's capital, has a very small city centre train station. The main train station is seven km from the centre of Pristina. The name of the station is Fushe Kosovë, which is the Albanian name for Kosovo because the Serbian words Kosovo Polje can lead to confusion, because it is also used as a name for the whole country. Strangely enough, Pristina's station is officially painted with cartoon characters on the city side. On the side of the rails are pictures of European railways, including an East German small town train station.

Pristina station

7.5 Romania

Iasi - the German castle

Romania only gained Transylvania and the Banat after the collapse of the Austro-Hungarian Empire at the end of World War I. Therefore, historic railway stations in this area are dominated by an Austro-Hungarian imperial architectural style. The older stations in other parts of the country, Moldavia and Wallachia, often have some German-style architectural features. This is partly because Romania was ruled between 1881 and 1947 by kings of the Hohenzollern-Sigmaringen dynasty. Due to its architecture, the train station in Iasi, Moldova, even had the nickname "German castle."

In August 1916, Romania changed alliance and joined the Allies in World War I. In the same month, the Central Powers (Germany, Austria-Hungary) occupied Bucharest and the south of the country. The Romanian government withdrew to Iasi in the north. But the country's treasury did not seem secure in the Moldova region either. There were plans to bring the state treasure to Denmark or England, but Romania feared that German submarines would attack them upon passage. Finally, an agreement was reached with the Russians to bring the state treasury to Moscow for safety. In December 1916, from the station of Iaşi, a train with seventeen wagons full of gold bars, coins, and jewels left for Moscow. In July 1917, another twenty-four wagons full of jewelry, precious paintings, and precious art objects followed. The Russian government signed a contract for the transport, storage, and return of these objects at 8 billion gold lei (current value: billions of Euros). However, the Russians never returned the Treasury. This soured Romanian and Russian relations and still affects Romania to this day.

★ Sinaia and the coat of arms

Of little German appearance is, however, the architecture of the railway station of Sinaia, which was formerly used by the Romanian king and his guests. The Romanian king hailed from the Hohenzollern branch of German royalty, and therefore, the Hohenzollern coat of arms can be seen above the portal of the station. The station is close to the Peles Castle: the former summer residence of the king. On the platform, there is a plaque that commemorates the Romanian Prime Minister Ion Duca. On 30 December 1933, he was murdered in the station by a zealous fascist guard. In the days of communism, there was a presidential train, in which U.S. President Gerald Ford and Romanian dictator Nicolae Ceausescu arrived here in August 1975.

Ploiesti-South Station

The fact that the oil town of Ploieşti, which was badly damaged in World War II, was once rich is evident from its southern station. Its portal is similar to the Union Station in Washington, which in turn is modelled after the Arch of Constantine in Rome. Romania, on the other hand, derives its name from the Romans, which once colonized the country.

Bucharest North Station

The Bucharest North Railway Station is the main station of the Romanian capital. The first station building was opened in 1872. At that time, the station was still called Targoviste Station, named after the adjacent street. However, another station, the Filaret Station in the south of Bucharest, which no longer exists, was the first station in the city in 1869. During the Second World War, the south wing of the North Railway Station was hit by Allied bombs but later rebuilt in the old style. A locomotive shed in the south of the train station was abandoned, and later on the land outside the station, the headquarters of the state railway company CFR were erected. In the post-communist period (after 1990), the station was a focal point for a major social issue in the country. To increase the population of Romania, Ceausescu had pursued a natalistic policy, which banned abortions and led to an increase in unwanted children. After the opening of the country, many adults also fled West, in turn, leaving their offspring. Suddenly, there was a large increase in children living on the streets, and long-distance trains brought desperate children from all over Romania to Bucharest. The main station became a sleeping place for homeless children. To restrict the use of the station for such purposes, access controls were introduced in the mid-1990s, and one could only enter the station with a valid ticket. The homeless children, therefore, moved to sewer and remote heat shafts beneath the streets in front of the station. They consoled themselves by sniffing the paint color Aurolac. Later on, Western humanitarian organizations came in to help, and an improved social system brought the number of homeless children down.

Bucharest Airport Station

In the fall of 2008, the Romanian Transport Minister announced that the Henri Coanda International Airport located in the Bucharest suburb of Otopeni could now also be reached by the metro. However, a real connection to the subway network in Bucharest is still several years away. What was opened was a new railway station with only one platform in the municipality Balotesti, 900 meters from the airport, which required a shuttle bus to reach. By the way, Balotesti was where dictator Ceausescu´s wife Elena

118

(executed in 1989) was born in 1916. In 1995, this community would have preferred being further away from the airport. A plane of the Romanian airline Tarom crashed in this community, and all 60 occupants died. The machine that crashed left a crater, not far from where the airport station is located today.

Burdenje - the legend of the German railway station

In the 19th century, the second-largest train station in Romania was built in Burdenje, a small town in the Romanian Moldavia that was shaped by a Jewish shtetl. Burdenje was a border station to Austria, and in the 19th century, the Romanian government wanted to build a representative building as a sign of their identity and strength. Trains from Vienna and Chernivtsi touched for the first time Romanian soil here. After its independence, Romania was ruled for a long time by the Hohenzollern kings, who were born in Sigmaringen, Germany. Therefore, there was a rumor that the design of the station also came from Germany. Even today, it can be read on many websites, the main building of Burdenje was a copy (on a smaller scale) of the railway station of Freiburg. However, the old Freiburg train station looked different and if Burdenje were a scaled-down version, Freiburg should have had the largest train station in Germany. The Romanian Wikipedia articles on Burdenje say that the station was modeled on the Swiss Fribourg station (Fribourg), but that is also not true. After World War II, the Bukovina and its river town Suceava became a part of Romania. Burdenje was a suburb of Suceava. Therefore, the station is referred to in railway timetables as Burdenje Suceava. After a renovation in 2000, the massive red brick building, with its round windows and arched doorway, is definitely one of the most beautiful train stations of Romania.

119

7.6 Bulgaria

Sofia and the tent roof

On August 1st, 1888, a historicist main station in the neo-Renaissance style was opened in Sofia. Yet, in April 1974, this beautiful station (built by French and Italian architects) was torn down to make way for a brutal looking new building. The socialist government wanted to leave its mark on the architecture of the capital and, at the same time, gain a large parading place in front of the station. However, after 1989, the rail traffic declined sharply, and this rapidly aging architectural design was not particularly popular among Bulgarians. After 2004, the emptiness of the station square was filled with a tent roof construction, which is reminiscent of the Munich Olympic Stadium, and further underlines the architectural movement towards more western designs. This architectural element is not entirely unsuitable because, like the new train station, the Olympic Center dates from the 1970s.

Burgas - the same in green

The port city of Burgas boasts that it has the most beautiful train station in Bulgaria. Yet, the station, which opened in the 1920s, looks the same as the station in the Bulgarian port of Varna. The only distinguishable feature is that the station of Varna is painted red, while Bourgas station is painted green (white, red, and green are the national colors of Bulgaria). The clockwork for the Varna station tower was installed in 1929. It had been specially procured from Germany.

★ Ankara train station - Ataturk's first stay

Kemal Ataturk, the father of modern Turkey, resided in the house of the stationmaster after he arrived in the new capital Ankara from 1919 to 1921. In this house, there was a telegraph station, which Atatürk made great use of to hold his country together. Ataturk's German-made railway car had special antennas for telegraph traffic.

Istanbul Sirkeci - East Europe

Located on the European side, Sirkeci station was once famous as the terminus of the Orient-Express. In the 1920s, a freight train from France brought clothing to Turkey every week. Kemal Atatürk wanted to bring his countrymen closer to Western-style attire. The station was opened in 1890, and the building looks oriental. This comes as no surprise since it was designed by the Prussian architect August Jachmund, who was sent by the German government to Istanbul to study oriental style architecture.

Istanbul Haydarpasa - Europe in Asia

The Haydarpasa train station on the Asian side looks more European. Again, this should come as no surprise because it was built by the company Philipp Holzmann after plans from the German architects Otto Ritter and Helmut Cuno. The castle-like station in the neo-Renaissance style was a gift from Kaiser Wilhelm II to Sultan Abdul Hamid of Turkey, an important ally of Germany. 1100 piles, each 21 meters long, had to be driven into the soft ground to create a stable foundation. The station is one of the few in the world surrounded on three sides by water.

Karaagac and the first bomber

In the First Balkan War (October 1912 - May 1913), Serbia, Montenegro, Bulgaria, and Greece fought against the Ottoman Empire. In this war, a Bulgarian pilot threw the first aircraft bomb (and, thus, became the first bomber pilot of history) at the station of Karaagac near Edirne. Karaagac lies on the western bank of the Evros (Turkish: Meric) River, which later formed the border with Bulgaria and then with Greece. Karaagaç remained as a suburb of Edirne in Turkey, but a new train station had to be built east of the river since the old Karaagaç train station was cut off from the rest of the country by the demarcation. The old, restored train station now houses a university, and the steam train parked on the tracks is now a restaurant.

Bursa's Acemler

The website of the Ministry of Culture and Tourism of Turkey reports the following anecdote relating to the Bursa Acemler station. When the Belgian Chemin de Fer de Moudania-Brousse opened the Bursa Acemler train station in 1892, the posted timetable showed the hours that were customary in Western European timekeeping. At that time, however, Turkey had its own time measurement, in which day and night were divided into 12 hours, the length of which changed according to the season. The railway company, therefore, put up a note in September 1892 to draw the passengers' attention to the fact that the timetables were based on Western European hours. But, eventually, the company had to give in to the habits of the local population and post the departure times in Turkish hours.

★ The orphan girl in the station of Bursa

In 1925, an orphan girl named Sabiha asked Atatürk if he could help her get into boarding school upon his arrival in Bursa. On 22 September 1925, the child-friendly Atatürk (he supposedly said that "Children are a new beginning and a new future") adopted Sabiha. In 1934, surnames became mandatory in Turkey, and Sabiha was called Gökcen (which means "belonging to heaven"). Sabiha was allowed to live with his three other adoptive daughters in his residence in Ankara. Later, the girls attended university in Istanbul. In 1935, when Turkey's first flight school opened, Sabiha showed enthusiasm for aviation and was allowed to go to Moscow, along with seven male students, to learn how to fly. In 1936, she went to the Turkish Air Force Academy. In 1937, she took part in a military operation and became the first fighter pilot, world-wide. She flew during the Korean War and was nicknamed "Amazon of the Skies." When the United States Air Force, published a poster titled "The 20 Greatest Aviators of History" in 1996, Gökcen was depicted as the only woman on it. Sabiha Gokcen died on 22 March 2001: her 88th Birthday. That same year, Istanbul's second airport, located on the Asian side (the airport in the European part is called Atatürk Airport), was named after Sabiha Gökcen.

8. Russia and Ukraine

8.1 Ukraine

Kiev's English Station

Kiev's first station was built in 1868-1870 in the English-Gothic style. The current station, which is the busiest in Ukraine with 170,000 passengers daily, also has a reference to England. Officially it is called "Kyiv Passazhyrskyi," but the population says "Voksal," which can also be read on the facade (in Cyrillic letters). Voksal is the Russian word for a larger railway station and is derived from the London borough of Vauxhall.

Lviv train station

Lviv's station, opened in 1904, is one of the most beautiful art nouveau influenced stations of Eastern Europe. After its opening, it was visited by many architects, and it influenced the architecture of Prague's main railway station and the S-Bahn stations of Vienna designed by Otto Wagner.

Podwolotschyska and roast goose

Podwolocyzyska, which belonged to Austria until 1918 and is located on the border with Russia, became an important transshipment point between southern Russia and Central Europe after closing a gap in the Russian rail network. Podwoloczyska was also the center of the egg trade, where egg prices for Europe were temporarily set at an egg exchange. In Podwolocyszka (now called Pidvolochysk), which was founded in 1900, the writer Hermann Kesten was born. Another Austrian writer, Alexander Roda Roda (1872-1945), helped the town's train station gain a certain level of literary fame through the story "Die Gans von Podwolotschyska (The Goose from Podwolotschyska)."

In this story, the station restaurant offers a small menu for four crowns (soup and beef) and a large menu for six crowns, which also includes goose and Zibebenstrudel. The passengers coming the long way from Vienna arrive hungry at this border station, would take a break, and choose the most expensive menu. But as soon as the diners have eaten the beef, a man with a service cap (this is the train station manager) comes into the restaurant and says, "It's time for the train to Kiev, Moscow, Odessa…" In response, everyone in the diner stands up and rushes to the rail cars without having savored the full menu. One day, however, the diners remained seated because they were a Lviv commission who were there to examine the Galician railway station management. In desperation, the innkeepers try to conjure up something to cook since they actually did not have any geese. When the inspectors then ask for the dessert, the host cunningly says Ziebebenstrudel (raisin strudel) is actually his last name and that corresponding item on the dining is not dessert, but rather his signature.

8.2 Russia (European part)

Voksal

The Russian word for a major railway station is Voksal, which derives from a London suburb called Vauxhall. For a precise connection, there are various theories. The most likely is that this is related to an amusement park at the terminus of the first railway of Russia built in 1837, which ran from Petersburg to Pavlovsk. The park was based on the then-famous Vauxhall Pleasure Gardens in London. Soon the word was on the station building itself and, later, became a general designation for larger stations.

West and east of Wershbolowo

One of the most magnificent railway stations in Russia used to be on the border with Germany: the Wershbolowo station. Here, different gauges came together (Russia had broad gauge of 1520 mm, Germany standard gauge of 1435 mm). Therefore, even the Tsar had to change here. Accordingly, the installations were of very refined standards. As Russia was considered backward compared to the West for a long time, there has long been the saying, "Everything is new only east of Wershbolowo, what is new here, is not new there (west)." After World War I, the station was located in Lithuania and thus called Virbalis. At the end of World War II, the station was only slightly damaged. The Russian troops had orders to blow up the nearby former German station of Eydtkuhnen (whose architecture is not bad either). However, as a result of a lack of local knowledge, they destroyed the magnificent railway station of Wershbolowo.

The first Russian station

The Vitebsk railway station was the first station in St. Petersburg and also in Russia. It was opened in 1837 and was originally called Tsarskoe Selo station because the trains from here went to the imperial summer residence. A replica of the first Russian campaign can be seen in the station. The station was later rebuilt in the Art Nouveau style and is still one of the most beautiful station buildings of St. Petersburg. Its intact historic atmosphere has led to Anna Karenina and Sherlock Holmes stories being filmed here.

The clocks of the Vitebsk Station

Despite the historical ambience, modern Swiss station clocks were hung in Vitebsk train station in 2003. This is surprisingly related to an airplane crash on Lake Constance. On the 1st of July, 2002 a Russian Tupolev from Bashkirian Airlines, which had schoolchildren on board, collided with a cargo plane at a height of 11,000 meters. All 71 passengers died. The accident was due to the failure of the Swiss air traffic controllers. The Russian media allegations led to a deterioration of the relationship between Russia and Switzerland. In 2003, Switzerland took advantage, however, of the 300th birthday of St. Petersburg to improve its image in Russia. The city was given 100 Swiss railway clocks, which were installed not only on pedestrian roads but also in train stations. This is also how the Vitebsk Station got Swiss railway clocks. But a Russian who had lost his wife and children in the accident, could not forget what happened. He traveled to Switzerland in February 2004 and stabbed the air traffic controller responsible for the accident at his private home.

St. Petersburg - Moscow railway station

In 1851, the first Russian long-distance railway line, the connection of the former capital of St. Petersburg to Moscow, was completed. The engineer was George Washington Whistler, an American. He chose the gauge of the track of his U.S. Southern home region, namely 1524 mm, which is exactly five feet. This broad gauge became the standard gauge in the Russian Empire. For the station in St. Petersburg, which sees itself as the Venice of the North, the architect chose Italian models. The arcades on the ground look Venetian, the first floor was inspired by a Tuscan palazzo, while the Clock Tower mimics the tower of the Palazzo Senatori in Rome. This St. Petersburg station is called Moscow railway station. At the other end of the track in Moscow, there is an identical copy. Today, however, this is not called St. Petersburg Railway Station, but, as since 1925, Leningrad Railway Station. There were plans for renaming, but they have not yet been realized.

Moscow Stations

In addition to the Leningrad Station, Moscow has eight other terminal stations (with a total number of passengers of almost two million per day). In Yaroslaw station, built in 1902-04 in a strange neo-Russian style and from which the Trans-Siberian railway departs, the Soviet Union still exists. On its roof are the hammer and sickle and the words CCCP (USSR).

☞ The Museum of Paweletski station provides further Soviet nostalgia. Here we find the funeral wagon, with which the corpse of Lenin was transferred from Gorky (now called again Nizhny Novgorod) to Moscow in 1924.

Moscow's Kiev Station

The clock tower of the Kiev railway station in Moscow is nicknamed Big Ben by the population because of its height and the great clock. Like St. Pancras in London, the train station also shares a huge glass platform hall. Moscow's Kiev Railway Station is the only long-distance rail courtyard of the capital whose facade faces the Moscow River.

★ Tolstoy's death

In November 1910, at the age of 82, the great Russian writer Leo Tolstoy (Lev Nikolayevich, Count Tolstoy) was travelling by train south with his doctor and his daughter. It is not clear where he wanted to go. Some thought he wanted to travel to the Caucasus mountains, while others thought to Constantinople. He contracted pneumonia on the train ride. After he spat blood, he had to leave the train at Astopowo station, several hundred kilometers south of Moscow, to interrupt the journey. He lay down in the station keeper's house and died there a few days later, surrounded by the press. Later, the station in the village was renamed Tolstoy train station. For the filming of Tolstoy's death in the 2008 film *The Last Station*, this was done not in Russia but at the station of Pretzsch in Saxony-Anhalt (Germany).

Samara - high and low

The new central station of Samara is considered the tallest railway station in Europe. It includes a more than 70 m high office tower. However, because of the vibrations of the train, the large glass panes had to be exchanged several times. When the Germans were advancing on Moscow, Stalin withdrew to Samara by train, because he had fear of flying. The city had the deepest bunkers of the Soviet Union. In May 2007, Samara was the location of the EU-Russia summit.

Kaliningrad, South Station

This station was opened in 1929 as a railway station of Königsberg. It was then considered the most modern station in Germany and was later used as the model for Duisburg Station. While little was left of the old Königsberg at World War II, the station survived unscathed. The tracks were, however, converted to broad gauge. Additionally, the station, like the city (now Kaliningrad), was renamed South Station. Soon after the political changes of post-1989, the first tourist special trains from Berlin arrived. Today, there is a daily train to Gdansk, with some wagons traveling through to Berlin.

Murmansk and Pechenga

Murmansk, the second northernmost city in the world after Norilsk (68 ° 58 '), has various records for the northern location of facilities (since the Norwegians expanded Longyearbyen, which is 10 degrees further north on Svalbard, it has some Northern records too). Murmansk has the northernmost synagogue and the northernmost ice-breaker. Perhaps Murmansk even has the northernmost train station in the world. Pechenga, north-west of Murmansk not far from the border with Norway, actually claims that title for itself. But it is not certain whether trains still leave there today.

★ Nureyev's birth

The birthplace of dancer Rudolf Nureyev (1938-1993) is sometimes given as Irkutsk, but that is only an approximate location. Nureyev's heavily pregnant Tatar mother wanted to be at birth alongside her husband, who was stationed as an officer of the Red Army in Vladivostok. Therefore, she set out on the Trans-Siberian railroad to the Pacific. Yet, during the train voyage, she began to give birth. Nureyev, the greatest dancer of the 20th Century, was (on 17 March 1938) born on a train, before it reached Irkutsk.

Yekaterinburg (Vokzal)

Yekaterinburg (Sverdlovsk from 1924 to 1991) is located just 40 km east of the Ural Mountains, which form the dividing line between Europe and Asia. The bridge between Asia and Europe is also evident in the train station, in which two allegorical figures represent Europe and Asia.

★ Yekaterinburg-Shartash

In the summer of 1918, the Russian royal family arrived at Shartash train station in Yekaterinburg from their place of exile: Tobolsk. The Bolsheviks wanted to avoid meeting the Czar at the main station because they wanted to settle things discreetly. On 17 July 1918, Tsar Nicholas II and his family were shot and killed, allegedly on the orders of Lenin.

Sludyanka - the marble station

The Sludyanka station of the Trans-Siberian railway is the only station in the world built of marble. Therefore, it got the nickname marble station. Near the town, there is a marble quarry. This marble is mainly used for gravestones. With the marble station, the state wanted to celebrate the progress of the construction of the Trans-Siberian railway. By the way, all stations on the Trans-Siberian railway show Moscow time on the station clock to help passengers gain a reference time.

Norilsk

Norilsk (210 000 inhabitants) is the northernmost major city in the world (69 ° 20 '). The town has no access to the Russian rail network. From 1949 to 1953, Stalin pushed for a Polar railway line, which, when finished, would have led to Igarka, near Norilsk. Because the construction took the lives of an average of ten workers every day, the project was soon nicknamed the "Railway of Bones." With Stalin's death, the project was abandoned. However, since the region is very resource-rich, there are plans to resume the construction of the unfinished railway line and to extend it to Norilsk.

Birobidzhan

In 1928, Stalin set up a Jewish Autonomous Region at the Chinese border. The capital is Birobidzhan, which was reached in 1898 by the Trans-Siberian Railway. Its station is the only one in the world that shows the city name in Cyrillic and Hebrew characters.

Novosibirsk

Built in the 1930s, the station of Novosibirsk is the largest of the Trans-Siberian Railway. That fact that steam locomotives were still used at the time of construction becomes evident in the facade. The station building looks like the profile of a steam locomotive.

Novosibirsk, Russia's third-largest city today, was founded in 1893 and was known until 1925 as Novonikolayevsk, named after the last Tsar.

Vladivostok

Since 1903, the Trans-Siberian railway links the Pacific city of Vladivostok with Moscow, 9288 rail kilometers away. The station of Vladivostok is a copy of the Yaroslavl train station in Moscow built 1902-1904 by Fyodor Schechtel, which is the starting point of the Trans-Siberian railway. After the Russian Revolution, the Communists sawed off the heads of the double eagle on the station facade. Vladivostok is not, as one might think, the most easterly station of the Trans-Siberian railway. It is only the southernmost. The easternmost station is Khabarovsk, named after the Cossack Khabarov.

Nakhodka

During the Cold War, Vladivostok was off-limits to foreigners. The ferries to Japan departed from the second endpoint of the Trans-Siberian route: the port of Nakhodka. The American writer Paul Theroux said in his 1975 travel book *The Great Railway Bazaar* that Nakhodka train station had stucco walls and the dimensions of the madhouse in Kabul.

9. Caucasus

Yerevan and the wedding-cake style

In 2000, readers of the British magazine *The Independent* asked travelers to nominate their favorite station in areas less frequented by tourists. David Turns from Liverpool suggested Bled Jezero station in Slovenia, Cincinnati Union Station in the U.S., and the main station of Yerevan in Armenia. Turns commented that Yerevan's station, with its large spire, stands out clearly in this city, where most buildings are flat due to the risk of earthquakes in the region. The station was built in 1956 and was one of the last buildings made in the Stalinist wedding cake style. The facade, with its colonnades and its pointed station tower, dominates the station square. Even a red star, obsolete today, can be seen at the station mast. However, the station is not very busy today. When Turns visited it, he was the only passenger in the train station and realized that only four trains departed from the station per day.

★ Gori and Stalin

Gori, Georgia, has a creamy yellow, well-preserved neoclassical station with a portico. Above the station platform side door, a portrait of Joseph Stalin hung for a long time. Additionally, a statue of Stalin could be found in one of the station's waiting areas up until a few years ago. The appreciation for the Soviet dictator, whose statue also stood in front of the town hall until 2010, was because he was born in Gori in 1878.

Gori is located near the border with South Ossetia and was occupied by Russians and South Ossetians in August 2008 during the armed conflict in Ossetia. Later, the Georgians tried to dismantle the Stalinist commemoration statue.

The airport train station in Tbilisi

Greek mythology tells of a fabulously rich country on the eastern edge of the Black Sea, in which Jason and the Argonauts kidnapped the Golden Fleece from King Aeëtes with the help of his daughter Medea. The Golden Fleece was the fur of the ram Chrysomeles, who could fly. The ram rescued the children of King Athamas from her jealous stepmother Colchis. The ram was sacrificed, and its fleece hung in a sacred grove, where it was guarded by a dragon. The location of the sacred grove is believed to be today's Georgia. Georgia was once rich with gold, and sheepskins were used to wash the gold from the rivers, which is one possible explanation for the Golden Fleece myth.

Visitors who arrive at the airport of the Georgian capital Tbilisi and take the train to the city center from the airport train station (which former President Mikheil Saakashvili once said was much better than the one from Geneva) may be reminded of this myth. This is due to the station's golden exterior cladding and curved shape, which looks as if someone had draped the Golden Fleece over the railway station.

Annex

1. Nicknames of railway stations

France

Haut Picardie (TGV)	Gare aux betteraves
Juvisy sur Orge	Largest station of the world
Lille Europe	Gare aux courants d´air
Paris Châtelet les Halles	Flipper
Perpignan	Spiritual centre of the world

Italy

Roma Termini	Il dinosauro (the dinosaur)
Roma Termini	Pope John II-Station (official)

Austria

St. Anton	St. Beton

Great Britain

London Paddington	Gateway to the West
London St. Pancras	Railway cathedral

Spain

Canfranc	Gare fantôme

Benelux

Antwerp Central	Railway cathedral
Den Haag C.S.	Sjoelbaak
Rotterdam CS	Patatzak (potato sack)

Central/Eastern Europe

Bratislava	Green house
Iași (Romania)	German chateau
Prague Hlavni nadr.	Wilson station, Hlavak
Sludjanka (Russia)	Marble station

2. Famous persons who died in railway stations

Person (Plaque ❖)	Station	Cause of death, Year
I.F. Annensky (Russian poet)	Tsarskoe Selo Bhf (RU)	*heart failure, 1909*
Leo Tolstoi ❖ (Russian writer)	Astopowo (RU)	*Tuberculosis, 1910*
Emile Verhaeren (Belgian poet)	Rouen (FR)	*Run over by a train, 1916*
Ion Duca (Romanian Prime Minister)	Sinaia (RO)	*Shot by fascists, 1933*
Attila Jozsef ❖ (Hungarian poet)	Balatonszarszo (HU)	*Run over by a freight train, 1937*
Zbigniew Cybulski ❖ (Polish actor)	Breslau (PL)	*hit by a train, 1967*

Other famous persons memorized by a plaque in the station

Person	Station	Event (statue/plaque)
Isambard Brunel (1806-1859)	London Paddington	*Important British rail engineer*
Salvador Dali (1904-1989)	Perpignan	*Inspired by the station (monument on the roof))*
Kazimierz Nowak (1897-1937)	Posen/ Poznan	*Polish Africa traveller*
James Joyce (1882-1941)	Ljubljana	*Spent one night at the station (plaque on the platform)*
John Betjeman (1906-1984), brit. Railway poet	London-St. Pancras	*Fought in the 1960s for the survival of rail lines*
	Dilton Marsh Halt	*Betjeman-poem at the station*

4. Special meeting pints at or in railway stations

Station	Meeting point
Glasgow Central Station	*Heilanman´s Umbrella* Station bridge over Argyle Street
Helsinki main station	Unter the lamp carrying giants at the entrance
Kopenhagen Hbf	*Under the clock "under uret"* At the large clock in the station hall
London Waterloo Station	*Waterloo Station Clock* Hanging clock in the station hall
Roma Termini	*Lampada Osram* High lamppost on the station square.
Stockholm	Circular opening "*Spottkoppen* (spittoon)" in the ground floor
St. Petersburg Moscow station	Statue of Peter the Great in the station hall
Zürich Main station	Large standing clock in the middle of the station concourse

5.Models for railway stations

Station	*Model*
Antwerpen CS	Inside: Pantheon in Rome Cuppola: Lucerne (old station)
Budapest Keleti Pu	Berlin old. Lehrter Station
Milano Centrale	Washington Union Station
Paris Gare de Lyon	Clock tower: Big Ben tower

6. Important European railway station architects

Architect	Stations
Friedrich Eisenlohr (1805-1854)	Lahr, Emmendingen und Denzlingen. first stations of Mannheim, Karlsruhe, Freiburg, Heidelberg. Style: neo-gothic
George Gilbert Scott (1811-1878)	London St. Pancras (1868-1877) Style: neo-gotisch
Friedrich Bürklein (1813-1872)	old station of Munich and Würzburg
Wilhelm von Flattich (1826-1900)	Wien Südbahnhof Main station of Trieste
Jakob Friedrich Wanner (1830-1903)	Zürich Hauptbahnhof (1865-1871) Aarau Bhf, Schaffhausen Bhf Style: Neorenaissance
Gustave Eiffel (1832-1923)	Budapest Nyugati, Maputo (Mosambique), Hall of Estacion Centr. (Santiago de Chile)
Frederick W. Stevens (1847-1900)	Bombay Victoria Station (1888) Style: Neogothic, oriental
Ferenc Pfaff (1851-1913)	Cluj-Napoca, Pecs, Miskolc Tisza, Rijeka, Zagreb main station
Ellel Saarinen (1873-1950)	Helsinki station (1910-14),Vyborg (1913), destroyed, Style: Art Nouveau
Paul Bonatz (1877-1956)	Stuttgart main station (1914-1927) Style: new Sachlichkeit
Meinard von Gerkan (1935)	Berlin main station (2006) Style: Modern functional
Santiago Calatrava (1951)	Zürich Stadelhofen (1984), Lissabon Oriente (1998), Airport station Lyon (1994) Liege-Guillemins (2007) Style: modern, biomorphic forms

7. The largest stations in Europe

Country	Passengers/visitors per working day (1000)
Belgium	Brüssel Central 400 (Reisende: 140), Midi 250, Nord 100; Leuven 55, Gent Sint Pieters 44, Antwerpen CS 39, Namur 38, Mechelen 19, Lüttich-G. 17, Mons 11, Charleroi 10
Bulgaria	Sofia Hbf 11 (passengers)
Denmark	Kopenhagen (passengers): main 80, Österport 30
Finland	Helsinki: 200, Pasila 50; Tampere 4.5
France	Paris: Gare du Nord 500, St. Lazare 250, Gare de Lyon 225, Montparnasse 140, Gare de L´Est 93, Austerlitz 68; Lyon Part Dieu 80, Lille 60, Straßburg 55, Bordeaux St J. 50, Nancy 40, Toulouse 22, Marseille 25, Metz 25, Rouen 14, Mulhouse 11
Great Britain	London: Waterloo 210, Victoria 169, St Pancras 146, Paddington 69; Birmingham New Street 95, Glasgow Central 93, Manchester Piccadilly 55, Leeds 50, Edinburgh 42, Belfast 25
Italy	Roma Termini 480, Milano Centrale 320, Turin P.N. 192, Florenz S.M.N 160, Bologna Centrale 159, Napoli Centrale 152, Venezia Mestre 85, Verona PN 68, Genua P. Principe 66, Palermo 52, Padua 50, Bari 38
Latvia	Riga 74 (passengers, 2006)
Netherlands	Amsterdam CS 150 (+100 visitors), Utrecht 145, Rotterdam 110, Leiden 80, Groningen 30, Gouda 19
Norway	Oslo 40
Poland	Lodz Fabrycna 17, Swinouscie 1
Romania	Timisoara 42, Bukarest Nord 40, Cluj Napoca 15, Iaşi 11, Craiova 10, Konstanza 6.5
Sweden	Stockholm 250, Göteborg 40, Uppsala 40, Malmö 38
Spain	Barcelona: Sants 124, Passeig de Gr. 41; Madrid Atocha 440, Malaga 66, Pamplona 6
Czechia	Prag Hlavni Nadr. 100, Brno 70

Literature

Les plus belles histoires des trains
Timée Editions, Boulogne 2003

Paul Atterbury
Tickets Please-
A Nostalgic Journey Through Railway Station Life
David & Charles, Shalbourne 2006

Bund Deutscher Architekten (Edit.)
Renaissance der Bahnhöfe
Vieweg Verlag, Braunschweig 1996

Jérôme Camand, Philip Gould (Photos)
Les Plus Belles Gares de France
La Vie du Rail, Paris 2005

Jean des Cars
Dictionnaire amoureux des Trains
Librairie Plon, Saint-Amand-Montrond 2006

Lis Künzli (Edit.)
Bahnhöfe. Ein literarischer Führer
Eichborn Verlag, Berlin 2007

Mihály Kubinsky
Bahnhöfe Europas- Ihre Geschichte, Kunst und Technik
Franck´sche Verlagshandlung, Stuttgart 1969

Benedict le vay
Britain from Rails
A Window Gazer's Guide
Bradt, Bucks (UK), 2009

Erich Preuß, Hans-Joachim Kirsche
Wunderwelt der Eisenbahn
GeraMond Verlag, München 2001

Ralf Roth
Das Jahrhundert der Eisenbahn
Jan Thorbecke Verlag, Ostfildern 2004

Brian Solomon
Railway Masterpieces
David &Charles, Newton Abbot 2002

Web sites

(für externe Links kann keine Verantwortung übernommen werden)

www.de.wikipedia.org
(Wikipedia-pages on various stations)

www.anecdotage.com
(American website on anecdotes)

www.jernhusen.se
(Data on Swedish stations)

www.kolej.one.pl
(Information on stations in Poland)

http://www.skyscrapercity.com/showthread.php?t=342415
World´s Largest and Busiest Rail Stations

http://www.kesten.de/index.php?station=podwol&kat=ORT
Information on Podwoloczyska **station**

http://rixke.tassignon.be/spip.php?article563
Mechelen, Milliaire-column near the station

http://www.treintrambus.be/actueel/blog/1216-opstapcijfers.html
Passenger stations in Belgium

http://www.ostpreussen.net/index.php?seite_id=12&bericht=04&kreis=13&stadt=23
Station Korschen (former East Prussia)

<u>Other railway station books of the author (in English)</u>
(See www.bod.de)
(in total 5 volumes, 1001 anecdotes and trivia on stations)

Palace of a thousand winds and the Gooseberry station
Short stories about 222 plus 2 stations in Germany
Books on Demand, Norderstedt 2020

The destiny station beyond the mountains
Short stories about 111 railway stations in the Alpine countries
Books on Demand, Norderstedt 2020

Grand Central Terminal and the station at the end of the world
Short stories about 222 train stations of the Americas, from Alaska to the Land of Fire
Books on Demand, Norderstedt 2020

Antwerpen CS